OECD Reviews of Vocational Education and Training

Pathways to Professions

UNDERSTANDING HIGHER VOCATIONAL AND PROFESSIONAL TERTIARY EDUCATION SYSTEMS

This work is published under the responsibility of the Secretary-General of the OECD. The opinions expressed and arguments employed herein do not necessarily reflect the official views of the Member countries of the OECD.

This document, as well as any data and map included herein, are without prejudice to the status of or sovereignty over any territory, to the delimitation of international frontiers and boundaries and to the name of any territory, city or area.

The statistical data for Israel are supplied by and under the responsibility of the relevant Israeli authorities. The use of such data by the OECD is without prejudice to the status of the Golan Heights, East Jerusalem and Israeli settlements in the West Bank under the terms of international law.

Note by Turkey
The information in this document with reference to "Cyprus" relates to the southern part of the Island. There is no single authority representing both Turkish and Greek Cypriot people on the Island. Turkey recognises the Turkish Republic of Northern Cyprus (TRNC). Until a lasting and equitable solution is found within the context of the United Nations, Turkey shall preserve its position concerning the "Cyprus issue".

Note by all the European Union Member States of the OECD and the European Union
The Republic of Cyprus is recognised by all members of the United Nations with the exception of Turkey. The information in this document relates to the area under the effective control of the Government of the Republic of Cyprus.

Please cite this publication as:
OECD (2022), *Pathways to Professions: Understanding Higher Vocational and Professional Tertiary Education Systems*, OECD Reviews of Vocational Education and Training, OECD Publishing, Paris, https://doi.org/10.1787/a81152f4-en.

ISBN 978-92-64-47478-9 (print)
ISBN 978-92-64-84843-6 (pdf)
ISBN 978-92-64-44845-2 (HTML)
ISBN 978-92-64-39517-6 (epub)

OECD Reviews of Vocational Education and Training
ISSN 2077-7728 (print)
ISSN 2077-7736 (online)

Photo credits: Cover © IR Stone/Shutterstock.com and Studio Folzer.

Corrigenda to publications may be found on line at: www.oecd.org/about/publishing/corrigenda.htm.
© OECD 2022

The use of this work, whether digital or print, is governed by the Terms and Conditions to be found at https://www.oecd.org/termsandconditions.

Foreword

As tertiary education has expanded, it has diversified both in respect of institutional missions and in forms of study. Higher vocational and professional tertiary programmes include a variety of programmes, such as associate degrees, higher technical programmes, professional bachelor qualifications and professional examinations. From a policy perspective, there are strong arguments for countries to monitor professional programmes and to benchmark their own experience against that of other countries, so as to develop their tertiary offer in a constructive way.

There is a policy debate about the best way in which to prepare people not only for a first job, but also a lifelong career and successful participation in society – and more broadly, about the type of education and training that can help achieve the desired mix of skills in an economy and society. It is sometimes argued that professionally-oriented programmes are most suited to ensure a smooth initial entry into the labour market. On the other hand, it is sometimes argued that programmes with more general orientation equip young people with sound generic skills, which will allow them to adapt to new requirements throughout their careers. This debate has no simple answer, but the first step is to establish reliable comparative data on how different countries prepare young people for the labour market.

The introduction of the International Standard Classification of Education 2011 framework opened the door to better data: countries may now report programmes with professional or academic orientation at all tertiary levels. Yet better data are still waiting on the doorstep because the current lack of internationally agreed definitions to underpin data collections undermines comparative analysis. Admittedly, the task is challenging: there is a continuum of programme orientations, and no classification maps neatly onto all national education and training systems, which are structured differently across countries. But agreeing on a pragmatic way of distinguishing by orientation would allow yield large returns, unlocking the potential of ongoing data collections regarding professional tertiary education.

This report compares the higher vocational and professional tertiary education sector across OECD countries, drawing on both quantitative and qualitative data. It describes types of programmes across countries and assesses data quality. It looks at pathways leading into professional programmes and transitions into further learning or the labour market, as well as the profile of learners served by professional programmes and links to the labour market. This report also seeks to improve the availability and quality of comparative data by advancing proposals to develop internationally agreed definitions of programme orientation at tertiary education levels to be used in future data collections.

This report was drafted by Viktória Kis and Simon Normandeau from the OECD Centre for Skills, under the supervision of Marieke Vandeweyer (manager of the VET team) and El Iza Mohamedou (head of the Centre for Skills). The report has benefited from comments provided by Mark Pearson (Deputy Director for Employment, Labour and Social Affairs), colleagues across the OECD, as well as the Group of National Experts (GNE) on VET. Administrative and editorial assistance was provided by Marie-Aurélie Elkurd and Jennifer Cannon from the OECD Centre for Skills.

This document was produced with the financial assistance of the European Union. The opinions expressed and arguments employed herein do not necessarily reflect the official views of the OECD member countries or the European Union.

Acknowledgements

Throughout the project, the OECD Secretariat received essential guidance and substantive input from the Ad hoc Working Group on Professional Tertiary Education. The authors are grateful to its members, who participated in meetings, provided comments on working documents and completed the OECD data collection on professional tertiary education. The authors are grateful to colleagues in the European Commission, who provided guidance and feedback throughout the project, in particular Chiara Riondino, Norbert Schoebel, Tim Schreiber and Kinga Szebeni. The report benefitted from the knowledge of several experts. Simon Field provided valuable input throughout the project as external expert, Denise Amyot, Slavica Černoša, Dietmar Eglseder, Cláudia Sarrico and Henno Theisens provided valuable input into the workshop conducted as part of the project. Hans Daale (Chain5) shared valuable insights throughout the project.

This project was conducted under the overall guidance of the Group of National Experts on Vocational Education and Training. We are also grateful to colleagues in the Indicators of Education Systems Working Party, the Network on Labour Market, Economic and Social Outcomes and the Group of National Experts on Higher Education for the opportunity to share emerging insights from our work with their members and benefit from their feedback. Within the OECD, the project and the draft report benefited greatly from comments of a number of OECD colleagues, including Éric Charbonnier, Marie-Hélène Doumet, Gara Rojas Gonzalez, Shinyoung Jeon, Małgorzata Kuczera, Simon Roy, Rodrigo Torres and Thomas Weko.

Table of contents

Foreword 3

Acknowledgements 4

Acronyms and abbreviations 8

Executive summary 9

1 Measuring professional tertiary education in comparative data 11
    Introduction 12
    The coverage of comparative data by level of tertiary education 16
    Towards internationally agreed definitions 35
    References 42
    Notes 45

2 Pathways into professional tertiary programmes 46
    Introduction 47
    Insights from comparative data 47
    Conclusion 61
    References 62

3 The profile of learners in professional tertiary programmes 64
    Introduction 65
    Insights from comparative data 65
    Conclusion 73
    References 74

4 Ensuring the relevance of professional tertiary programmes 75
    Introduction 76
    Insights from comparative data 77
    Conclusion 93
    References 95
    Notes 96

5 Key findings and proposals for the classification of tertiary programmes by orientation 97
    Note 100

Annex A. Background information on country inputs 101

FIGURES

Figure 1.1. Share of younger and older adults with a short-cycle tertiary qualification (2019) — 13
Figure 1.2. Share of younger and older adults with a professional bachelor's or equivalent professional qualification (2019) — 14
Figure 1.3. Academic or professional? Current classification for selected occupations — 17
Figure 1.4. Distribution of students by programme orientation at short-cycle tertiary level (2018) — 21
Figure 1.5. Distribution of students by programme orientation at bachelor's or equivalent level (2018) — 25
Figure 1.6. Distribution of students by programme orientation at master's or equivalent level (2018) — 30
Figure 2.1. Share of upper secondary students graduating from a vocational programme (2018) — 48
Figure 2.2. Distribution of students enrolled in upper secondary VET by access to tertiary education — 49
Figure 2.3. Distribution of new entrants by tertiary level (2018) — 52
Figure 2.4. Distribution of educational attainment of students in short-cycle tertiary programmes (2017-2019 pooled) — 53
Figure 2.5. Distribution of educational attainment of students in ISCED level 6 programmes (2017- 2019 pooled) — 53
Figure 2.6. Relationship between the share of graduates from upper secondary vocational programmes and their share in the entrance cohort at bachelor's level (2017) — 54
Figure 2.7. Share of short-cycle tertiary students with employment experience (2017-2019 pooled) — 57
Figure 2.8. Latest occupation held by ISCED 5 students with a VET background (2017-2019 pooled) — 57
Figure 2.9. Share of ISCED level 6 students with employment experience (2017-2019 pooled) — 58
Figure 2.10. Latest occupation held by ISCED level 6 students with a vocational background (2017-19 pooled) — 59
Figure 2.11. Latest occupation held by ISCED level 6 students with a general education background (2017-2019 pooled) — 59
Figure 2.12. Completion rate of ISCED level 6 students (2017) — 60
Figure 2.13. Share of young people with weak literacy skills, by programme orientation (2012, 2015 or 2017) — 61
Figure 3.1. Age distribution of short-cycle tertiary students (2018) — 66
Figure 3.2. Age distribution of professional bachelor's or equivalent students (2018) — 67
Figure 3.3. Mean age of students enrolled in bachelor's or equivalent level, by programme orientation (2018) — 67
Figure 3.4. Share of full-time and part-time students in short-cycle tertiary programmes (2018) — 68
Figure 3.5. Share of part-time students in bachelor's or equivalent level, by programme orientation (2018) — 69
Figure 3.6. Share of women enrolled in short-cycle tertiary and in professional ISCED level 6 programmes (2018) — 70
Figure 3.7. Share of women enrolled in selected fields of study (2018) — 71
Figure 3.8. Share of tertiary graduates with at least one tertiary-educated parent — 73
Figure 4.1. Distribution of work experience during tertiary studies (2016) — 84
Figure 4.2. Type of work-based learning experience during tertiary studies (2016) — 85
Figure 4.3. Distribution of graduates by field of study at short-cycle tertiary and bachelor's or equivalent level (2018) — 86
Figure 4.4. Relationship between the share of short-cycle tertiary new entrants and relative earnings, by field of study (2017) — 87
Figure 4.5. Employment rate of tertiary-educated adults relative to adults with upper secondary education (2019) — 88
Figure 4.6. Earnings of tertiary-educated adults relative to adults with upper secondary education (2018) — 89
Figure 4.7. Employment rate by work experience during tertiary studies (2016) — 89
Figure 4.8. Share of workers working more than 50 hours per week, by tertiary educational attainment (2012, 2015 or 2017) — 92
Figure 4.9. Mean literacy score by level of educational attainment (2012, 2015 or 2017) — 93

TABLES

Table 1.1. The position of vocational or professional programmes in European countries — 18
Table 1.2. Sources of comparative data on professional tertiary education — 19
Table 1.3. Short-cycle tertiary qualifications — 22
Table 1.4. Type of institutions delivering tertiary programmes — 34

Table 2.1. Professional programmes as a path from VET into academic programmes — 50
Table 4.1. The use of work-based learning in short-cycle tertiary education — 80
Table 4.2. The use of work-based learning in professional programmes at ISCED level 6 — 81

Table A A.1. Countries' input into the project "Higher VET – Professional tertiary education" — 101
Table A A.2. Academic or professional? Current classification for selected occupations — 102

Acronyms and abbreviations

AVS	Attestation of vocational specialisation
BES	Associate degree (Brevet d'enseignement supérieur)
BHS	Higher vocational school (Berufsbildende höhere Schule)
BTS	Higher technician's certificate (Brevet de technicien supérieur)
Cedefop	European Centre for the Development of Vocational Training
CEGEP	General and professional education college (Collège d'enseignement général et professionnel)
CQP	Professional qualification certificate (Certificat de qualification professionnelle)
CTeSP	Higher professional technician course (Curso técnico superior profissional)
DUT	University technology degree (Diplôme universitaire technologique)
EAG	Education at a Glance
ECTS	European Credits Transfer System
EQF	European Qualifications Framework
ESCO	European Skills, Competences, Qualifications and Occupations
EU	European Union
EU-LFS	European Union Labour Force Survey
GNE	Group of National Experts
HAVO	Senior general secondary education
HBO	University of Applied Sciences (Hoger beroepsonderwijs)
HEI	Higher education institution
INES	Indicators of Education Systems programme
ISCED	International Standard Classification of Education
ISCO	International Standard Classification of Occupations
LSO	Network on Labour Market, Economic and Social Outcomes of Learning
MBA	Master of Business Administration
OECD	Organisation for Economic Co-operation and Development
PIAAC	Programme for the International Assessment of Adult Competencies
STEM	Science, technology, engineering, and mathematics
UAS	University of Applied Sciences
UNESCO	United Nations Educational, Scientific and Cultural Organization
UOE	UNESCO / OECD / Eurostat
VET	Vocational education and training

Executive summary

As tertiary education has expanded over the past decades, it has also diversified, including programmes with very different designs and functions, ranging from two-year programmes in tertiary institutions to free-standing professional examinations designed to upskill existing practitioners. Tertiary institutions have also diversified, for example in the very different missions of traditional universities and universities of applied science. In some European countries the scale of enrolment in the professional sector of tertiary education now rivals that in regular universities. But not all countries have established a separate professional tertiary sector, in some countries, including the United States, similar applied, practically-oriented programmes like business studies or culinary arts are taught within multi-purpose institutions alongside programmes focused on single academic disciplines, like physics or history.

Against this background, there is debate about the type of education and training that can help achieve the desired mix of skills in an economy and society. Learners not only need the skills and qualifications to find a first job, but also the capacity to adapt to changing circumstances for a lifelong career and participation in society. For tertiary programmes, the question arises about the proportion of programmes that should take their point of departure as a target occupation as opposed to an academic field. While there is no simple answer, the first step is to monitor what countries are doing in this area and improve the quality of comparative data to allow for benchmarking and research. This project was therefore launched to help improve comparative data on professional tertiary education and to inform policy making. This report compares professional tertiary education across OECD countries, drawing on qualitative and quantitative data, and sets out proposals for the development of internationally agreed definitions.

Professional programmes come in many shapes and forms

Professional programmes, also called "higher VET" in some countries, exist in diverse forms, such as short-cycle tertiary programmes (mostly two-year programmes), professional examinations designed to upskill experienced practitioners, and professional bachelor programmes. They often differ strongly in terms of their function, the learners they serve and design:

- Professional programmes play a key role in upskilling VET graduates. They are sometimes the only type of tertiary education directly accessible from upper secondary VET, and in some cases they provide a bridge into "academic" higher education, thus facilitating permeability.
- Past or current work experience is common among tertiary students, especially among those with a vocational upper secondary background, who are also more likely to have held high-skilled jobs than those with a general education background.
- Younger adults dominate in programmes providing initial preparation for labour market entry, both short-cycle tertiary programmes and professional bachelor's programmes in various European countries. Other programmes, such as professional examinations, are especially designed for the upskilling of adults.

- Work-based learning is commonly an element in professional tertiary programmes especially at ISCED level 5, but is not always mandatory. Professional bachelor programmes often include mandatory internships and 'dual' tertiary programmes have also been growing. Relevant past or current work experience is often recognised as a form of work-based learning. Adults who benefited from work-based learning during their tertiary studies tend to have higher employment rates than those who did not, with longer (6 months and above) paid work placements leading to the best outcomes in terms of employment.

Internationally-agreed definitions will facilitate benchmarking and research

Huge gaps remain in comparative data because there are no internationally agreed definitions for programme orientation at tertiary level. For ISCED level 5, data are collected based on the agreed definition of "vocational". But for ISCED level 6 and above, countries that provide data do so based on their own national definitions. Therefore, programmes preparing for the same professions (e.g. teachers, nurses) are classified differently by countries. Some countries choose not to provide data in the absence of agreed definitions.

Two major grey zones arise in the classification of programmes. Some programmes are both "academic" (in the sense of highly demanding intellectually) and "professional" (in that they prepare for a particular profession) – examples include teachers and medical doctors. In addition, programmes that prepare for a broader economic or occupational sector (e.g. business studies, food technology) are also classified differently by different countries.

To help improve data availability and quality, building on ISCED 2011 and previous international discussion, this report makes proposals for the development of internationally agreed definitions covering the orientation of tertiary programmes. These are based on consultation with countries to provide an understanding of how programmes with different orientations are provided across countries, and the practical constraints they face for data collections.

The proposal is to establish a three-way classification:

- Type 1: Programmes that provide applied education and training designed to equip students with knowledge and skills required to practice a particular profession.
- Type 2: Programmes that provide applied education and training designed to equip students with the knowledge and skills required to work within an occupational family or industrial sector.
- Type 3: Programmes that provide discipline-oriented education in the pure sciences, humanities and arts. While such programmes should also provide knowledge and skills of labour market relevance, these are applicable in very diverse contexts and are not intended to prepare students for a particular profession, occupational family or industrial sector.

The terminology used for each category is to be agreed in consultation with countries to take into account the different nuances and resonances of particular terms in different languages. One option might be to refer to the categories below as "profession-oriented", "sector-oriented" and "general".

Additional indicators could complete this classification, to capture variation in the delivery of programmes and their quality. Examples of such indicators are the share of practical training (in real or simulated work environments), the share of work-based learning (in real workplaces) or the engagement of employers.

In addition, agreeing on the classification of detailed fields of study set out in the ISCED-F framework could help to ensure clarity regarding some numerically large programmes (e.g. teaching, nursing) and facilitate reporting in countries that lack the institutional or programmatic distinctions that could underpin classification.

1 Measuring professional tertiary education in comparative data

Professional tertiary education is a key component of country skills systems. This report compares this sector across OECD countries, drawing on both qualitative and quantitative data. This chapter introduces the report by describing the diverse forms of the sector in different countries, including, for example, short-cycle tertiary education; professional examinations designed to upskill experienced practitioners, and professional bachelor's programmes at level 6. Currently our data on this type of provision have major gaps, because of the lack of internationally agreed definitions. This chapter proposes a three-way classification to resolve this problem, distinguishing first, programmes that prepare students for a particular profession, second, programmes that prepare students to work within an occupational family or industrial sector, and third, programmes in the pure sciences, humanities and arts. The chapter concludes by setting out a set of practical tools to implement this proposal and thereby improve data availability.

Introduction

The diversification of tertiary education

The connection between universities and professional education and training is hardly new in history. In the Middle Ages some types of professional training took place in universities. Universities in Europe in the 13th century were expected to teach not only the "Seven Liberal Arts", but also law, medicine or theology (Rait, 1918[1]). However, by the middle of the 19th century, universities became focused on liberal education and pure research, leaving professional preparation outside their walls. The emergence of "modern" higher education towards the second half of the 19th century and the early 20th century produced a shift from small, homogeneous universities to a diversified and increasingly professional system of higher-level learning (Jarausch, 1982[2]). In the 19th century, various countries established institutions with a professional focus (e.g. polytechnique in Canada, university-based professional schools in the United States). In the 20th century and particularly accelerating over the decades following World War II, the purpose of higher education as preparation for specific professions became embedded in new types of programmes and institutions (Lazerson, 2013[3]). New types of higher education institutions, such as universities of applied sciences and polytechnics, emerged in many European countries with less focus on research and more on applied learning (Teichler, 2002[4]). Even in countries that maintained or moved to a unified higher education system, such as Australia, New Zealand, the United Kingdom or the United States, the expansion of higher education and the diversification of student body was accompanied by increasing sensitivity to labour market needs (McInnis, 1995[5]; Lazerson, 2013[3]).

In response to these developments, many tertiary programmes have become increasingly connected to employment opportunities. At bachelor's level, many countries have developed programmes focusing on applied, occupationally-oriented learning, offered either in a separate tier of institutions or within multi-purpose higher education institutions. In the United States, for example, undergraduate education shifted from a focus on arts and sciences to occupational-professional degrees over the second half of the 20th century (Brint et al., 2005[6]). Some countries have established designated professional bachelor's programmes targeting specific professions or occupational fields.

The diversification included also the development of shorter education and training programmes, as many of the emerging occupations required less than a traditional three- or four-year university qualification. For example, in the medical field programmes were established for medical assistants, physical therapists and radiological technicians. In the legal domain, programmes emerged to train paralegals and legal secretaries, while the field of engineering developed offers for engineering technicians (Lazerson, 2013[3]). Such shorter programmes leading to such "sub-degree" or "sub-bachelor" qualifications have greatly contributed to the expansion of higher education in the United Kingdom (Schuller, 1995[7]) and the United States (Lazerson, 2013[3]). These short-cycle tertiary programmes have often become not only a route to an entry-level job, but also a stepping stone into further learning at bachelor's level.

Another sector of the tertiary professional landscape evolved from upper secondary vocational education and training (VET), rather than from traditional university education, and is sometimes associated with crafts and trades with a long history of "Meister" qualifications. Several countries have developed programmes that provide a way for upper secondary vocational students to deepen their skills and knowledge. These take the form of one-or two-year programmes or qualifications based on an examination (e.g. master craftsman examinations, professional examinations).

Even over the past two decades, applied and professional programmes grew in several European countries, contributing to the increase in tertiary attainment of young adults across Europe. A study of "higher VET" in Europe (Ulicna, Luomi Messerer and Auzinger, 2016[8]) found that between 2000 and 2013 participation in these programmes grew in 12 countries, remained stable in six countries and decreased in nine countries. For example, enrolment in higher vocational programmes grew by 39% in Spain and by 25% in the French speaking community of Belgium. Programmes provided by universities of applied sciences grew also substantially in many countries, with an increase in enrolment by 112% in Austria, 29% in the Netherlands and 17% in Belgium-Flanders, while growth occurred also in professional higher education in Estonia (30%) and dual study programmes in Germany (57%). Box 1.1 complements the picture by providing some insights on the evolution of professional programmes over the past decades, comparing the highest qualification attained by adults of different ages[1]. The data are based on the International Standard Classification of Education (ISCED) and refer to the highest qualification of adults. For example if graduates of ISCED 5 programmes progress more often to ISCED 6, then ISCED 5 as highest attainment will become less common even if participation remained unchanged.

Box 1.1. Changes over time: Professional attainment among younger and older adults

In several countries short-cycle tertiary education has expanded (e.g. Korea, Spain), but in many countries short-cycle tertiary education remains very uncommon (e.g. Belgium, the Czech Republic, Germany, Iceland and Mexico).

Figure 1.1. Share of younger and older adults with a short-cycle tertiary qualification (2019)

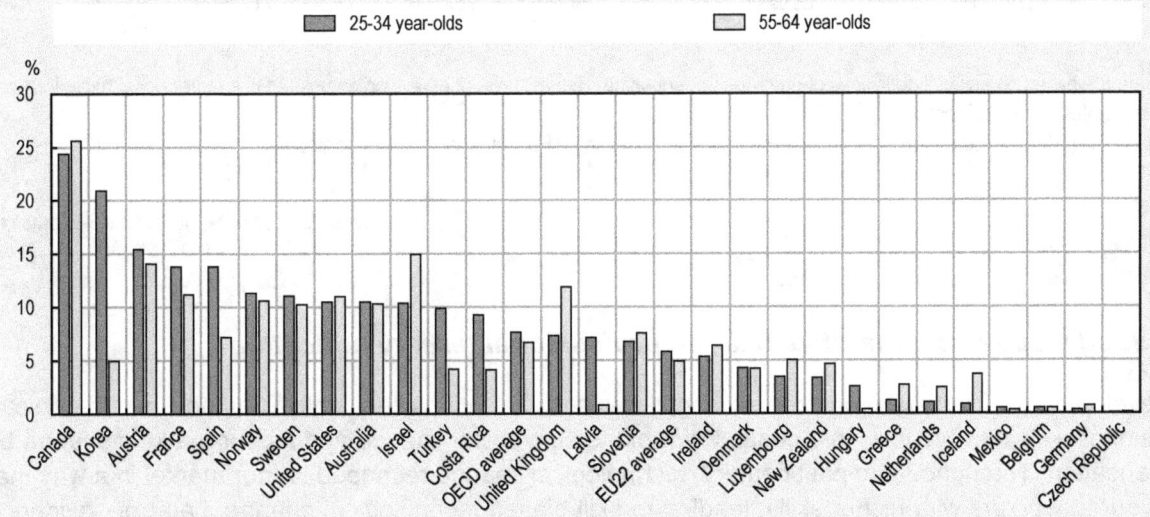

Note: Highest level of education completed is a short-cycle tertiary qualification, regardless of programme orientation.
Source: OECD (2021[9]), "Education at a Glance", Education and Training – Education at a Glance (database), https://stats.oecd.org/

StatLink https://stat.link/g9uend

In most countries with data, holding a professional ISCED 6 qualification has become more common. Such qualifications are held by at least 15% of young adults in Denmark, Greece, Lithuania, Mexico and the Netherlands. The Netherlands has the highest share of younger adults with a professional ISCED 6 qualification (24%), following the rapid growth in universities of applied sciences (HBO).

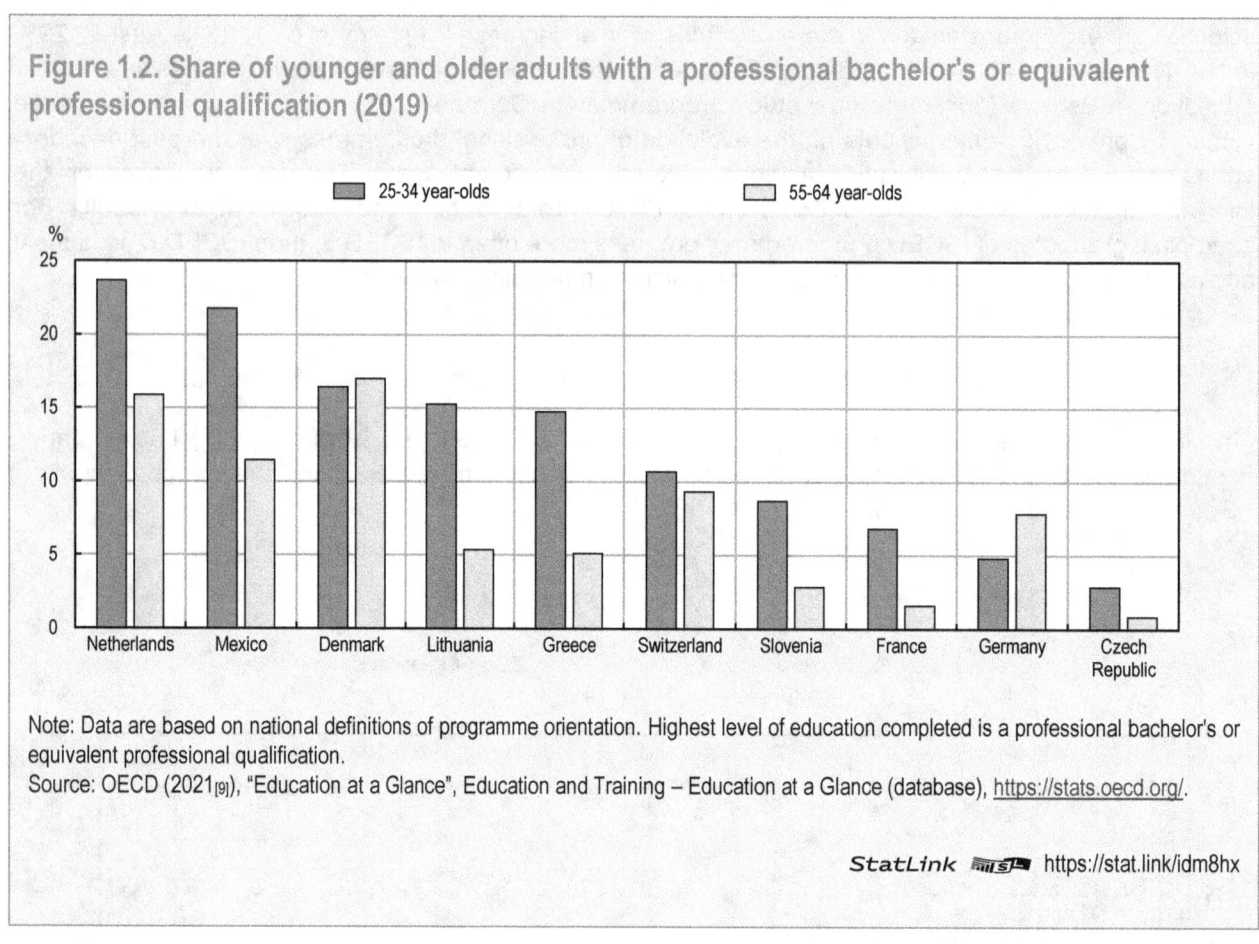

Figure 1.2. Share of younger and older adults with a professional bachelor's or equivalent professional qualification (2019)

Note: Data are based on national definitions of programme orientation. Highest level of education completed is a professional bachelor's or equivalent professional qualification.
Source: OECD (2021[9]), "Education at a Glance", Education and Training – Education at a Glance (database), https://stats.oecd.org/.

StatLink https://stat.link/idm8hx

The added value of comparative data on professional tertiary education

The development of tertiary programmes and dedicated institutions that deliver higher level technical, professional skills has occurred in a context of rapid technological change and labour markets shaped by job polarisation. Throughout the past century, technological change reshaped labour market in a way that has favoured workers with higher skills, leading to skill-biased technological change. Later on, evidence emerged of a distinction between how routine and non-route tasks are affected: routine tasks are increasingly replaced by automation, leading to routine-biased technological change. As a result of these trends, job polarisation has been observed for several decades, with jobs requiring mid-level skills becoming less important in labour markets, alongside growth in both occupations with high skills requirements (e.g. engineers, medical doctor) and in those with low skill requirements (but difficult to automate, such as providing basic care for the elderly). According to projections from Cedefop and Eurofound (2018[10]), job polarisation is expected to continue over the next decade. Forecasts suggest that employment growth will be strongest for professionals, technicians and associate professionals. Employment for managers, service and sales workers, and elementary occupations will grow but more slowly. By contrast, employment in occupations that might be considered "middle skilled" is expected to fall – this includes craft and related trades workers, clerks and skilled agricultural workers (OECD, 2020[11]).

Across OECD countries, automation is expected to replace 14% of jobs in the coming years and significantly reshape another 32%. The new jobs created will also have different skills requirements from those that disappear (OECD, 2019[12]). There are multiple implications for skills systems. First, initial education and training programmes can no longer be designed to prepare for an occupation that a person would pursue throughout their entire career. Education and training systems must ensure that individuals are equipped with the skills needed to pursue further learning. This is particularly important for vocational education and training systems, which used to be designed to prepare for jobs rather than further learning and have often neglected generic skills, in particular literacy and numeracy. Second, skills systems must provide suitable learning opportunities to those seeking advanced occupational skills, including adults who need to upskill or reskill. Programmes need to be organised in an adult-friendly way, allowing adults to build on their previous experience, fill any specific gaps in their skill set and pursue studies in a way that is compatible with other demands on their time (e.g. work, care responsibilities).

Several countries turn to tertiary programmes with a focus on applied learning and close connection to the labour market to deliver this – such programmes are sometimes part of a distinct sector referred to as "higher vocational education and training" or professional tertiary or higher education. Countries often view such programmes as an important means of widening access to tertiary education, engaging graduates of upper secondary VET programmes and more broadly, non-traditional tertiary students.

Against this background, there is a major policy debate about the best way in which to prepare people for not only a first job, but also a lifelong career and successful participation in society – and more broadly, about the type of education and training that can help achieve the desired mix of skills in an economy and society. When entering the labour market, all young people need skills and qualifications to find a first job. An initial smooth transition is important as it tends to have a long-term impact on career prospects (e.g. (Gregg and Tominey, 2005[13]; Möller and Umkehrer, 2014[14]; Ayllón, Valbuena and Plum, 2021[15])). Moreover, some labour market trends, including growth in outsourcing and temporary work, reduce incentives for employers to provide on-the-job training, particularly for those in entry-level jobs. As a result, there is an increasing need for the initial education and training system to equip young people with specific professionally-oriented skills, as well as general education. A practical approach, often including work-based learning, can help develop not only specific, technical skills but also broad employability skills, like teamwork and communication. Employers across Europe view a combination of professional (or sectoral) and interpersonal skills as essential when considering the recruitment of recent higher education graduates (Cedefop, 2014[16]).

On the other hand, it is sometimes argued that it is best to prepare young people for work and life with general education, rather than vocational or professional training. Such general education is designed to develop sound generic skills and ensure individuals have the capacity to adapt to changing circumstances, needed both to pursue a successful career and to function in society. The argument is that more specific knowledge and skills can then be acquired post-qualification and on the job (for a review of the literature on this debate see (Biewen and Thiele, 2020[17])).

In practice, programmes come in shades of grey, rather than black and white: all professional programmes need a large measure of general education, in particular literacy and numeracy, while general and academic programmes also develop skills that are of labour market relevance. But the broad question remains about the proportion of tertiary education programmes that should take a target occupation (or target occupations) as their point of departure and the proportion that should remain in more academic fields. There is no easy answer to this debate, but the first step is to monitor what countries are doing in this area, to improve the quality of comparative data to allow for analysis and research.

Comparative data can also shed light on the role of professional programmes in national skills systems. In some countries higher VET or professional tertiary education is viewed as a key tool to open access to tertiary education to graduates of upper secondary VET, students from lower socio-economic backgrounds and facilitate the massification of tertiary education. One of the objectives of the European Education Area is to increase the share of 30-34 year-olds with tertiary education to 50% by 2030 – professional programmes can help achieve this target by attracting those most interested in applied forms of learning.

This project was launched to help improve comparative data on professional tertiary education and to inform policy making in this area through better data. Box 1.2 describes the objectives and the methodology of the project.

> **Box 1.2. About the project: Higher VET – professional tertiary education**
>
> **Objectives**
>
> The objectives of the project were to inform policy development in the area of tertiary programmes with professional orientation based on international experience; explore possibilities to enhance the coverage of professional programmes in existing and future data collections; and stimulate dialogue on an international definition and classification of tertiary programmes by orientation.
>
> The scope of the project includes programmes at ISCED levels 5-7, with most of the analysis focusing on ISCED 5 and 6 programmes.
>
> **Methodology**
>
> The work has involved:
>
> - **Desk-based analytical work**: reviewing available evidence on country systems, policy and practice, assessing the quality of comparative data (e.g. OECD Survey of Adult Skills (PIAAC), data collected through the Indicators of Education Systems (INES) Working Party and its networks, European Union Labour Force Survey) and analysing comparative data.
> - **Dialogue with countries through the Ad hoc Working Group on Professional Tertiary Education**: Countries and international organisations (members of the Group of National Experts (GNE) on VET, the Higher Education GNE, the INES Working Party and the Network on Labour Market, Economic and Social Outcomes (LSO) were invited to join this group to discuss key policy issues, enrich the project with information on professional programmes across OECD countries and discuss issues regarding potential internationally agreed definitions for programme orientation at tertiary level. 27 countries and six international organisations joined the group.
> - **Data collection on professional tertiary education**: OECD member countries and key partners, as well as non-OECD EU member states and candidate countries, were invited to complete a questionnaire, composed of two parts. Part A sought to complement existing information in ISCED mappings and earlier surveys, with a view to explore the workability of potential internationally agreed definitions for programme orientation. Part B sought to collect examples of policy and practice in the area of professional tertiary education. 37 countries completed the questionnaire.
>
> The summary of country participation in the Ad hoc Working Group on Professional Tertiary Education is provided in Annex A (Table A A.1).

The coverage of comparative data by level of tertiary education

This section describes the programmes and qualifications currently covered by comparative data on professional tertiary education.

Professional programmes under the ISCED 2011 framework

The basis for the identification of professional tertiary programmes in comparative data is the International Standard Classification of Education (ISCED) 2011 framework. It allows for the identification of professional programmes at all tertiary levels, but its potential has not been fully realised. Under the earlier framework (ISCED 97), tertiary education was identified at levels 5 and 6. Level 6 was reserved for advanced research qualifications, such as Ph. D programmes, so the vast majority of tertiary programmes, including those at master's level, were at level 5, subdivided into 5A and 5B. 5B programmes were defined as being "practically oriented/occupationally specific" and "is mainly designed for participants to acquire the practical skills, and know-how needed for employment in a particular occupation or trade or class of occupations or trades" (UNESCO, 2006[18]). Despite this last definition, under ISCED 1997, ISCED 5A included not only more theoretical studies in the pure sciences and humanities, but also longer training programmes for professions such as medicine and architecture that have "high skills requirements". This left ISCED 5B, uncomfortably, covering professional programmes other than those with high status.

ISCED 2011 sought to resolve this issue through greater disaggregation of different levels of tertiary education, and by allowing that at each of these levels, programmes might have a different "orientation", with proposed categories of orientation being "professional" or "academic". ISCED 2011 offers four tertiary levels: short cycle tertiary (ISCED 5), and the three "Bologna" categories: bachelor's (ISCED 6), masters (ISCED 7) and doctoral (ISCED 8). Orientation is identified in the second digit of ISCED's 3-digit coding, so that, for example, a bachelor's degree is coded as 64 if academic, 65 if professional, and 66 if orientation is unspecified (UNESCO, 2012[19]). As professional programmes are available at all tertiary levels, the characteristic of being professional has no implication for the status or length of the programme.

But a major difficulty remains, in that there are not, as yet, internationally agreed definitions of "academic" or "professional" that would underpin the collection of comparative data. For ISCED level 5 it has been agreed to use the definition adopted for "vocational" programmes at lower ISCED levels. For ISCED levels 6 and above countries have been able to report a breakdown by orientation based on their own definitions of "professional" and "academic" or report programmes as having "unspecified orientation". One consequence is weak comparability: as illustrated by Figure 1.3, programmes preparing students for the same occupation are reported as academic in some countries, as professional or having "unspecified orientation" in others. While some of the variation may reflect real differences in the way in which individuals are prepared for the same professions in different countries, an undetermined and potentially large proportion of the variation involves unmeasured differences in definitional approaches. The implications for data coverage and quality at each ISCED level are discussed in the next section.

Figure 1.3. Academic or professional? Current classification for selected occupations

Orientation attributed to programmes leading to selected occupations in international data collections

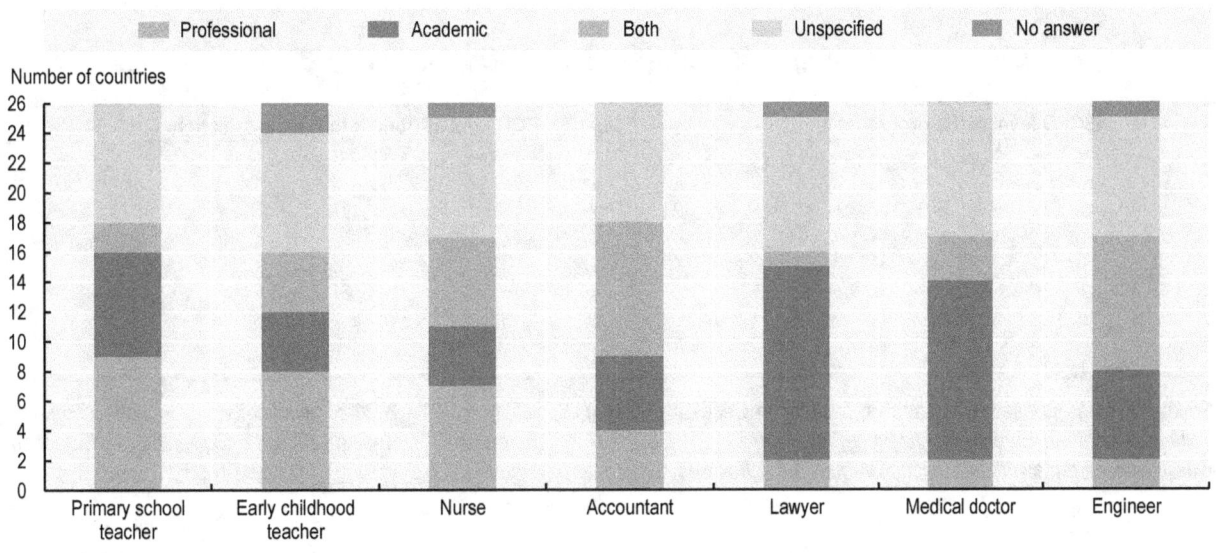

Source: OECD Data collection on professional tertiary education.

StatLink https://stat.link/gt6hra

An additional limitation of data collected under the ISCED framework is that they do not cover qualifications delivered outside the formal education and training system. In some countries such programmes (e.g. industry-led certifications) play a major role in preparing for advanced, technical occupations. For example, in the United States, examinations for master plumbers lead to a certificate of licensure, but not a formal educational qualification (similarly to the apprenticeship system, which is also outside the formal education system). Some certifications are developed by large companies or groups of companies (e.g. certification by Cisco or Caterpillar). Similarly, France has a large system of professional qualification certificates (CQP-s), which are part of a national register but are not considered formal education. Such industry-led certifications are very often not captured in comparative data – they are included only when a programme leads to both a formal qualification and an industry-recognised certification.

Recognising that the European Qualifications Framework (EQF) is commonly used as a reference for policy making and research in Europe, Box 1.3 describes the relationship between the two frameworks.

Box 1.3. The relationship between ISCED and EQF levels

The European Qualifications Framework (EQF) and the ISCED frameworks focus on different constructs and play different roles. The ISCED framework is designed to classify education and training programmes. The EQF is a reference framework for qualifications. It focuses on learning outcomes (knowledge, skills and competences), which may be achieved through different paths, including formal programmes, non-formal and informal learning. While there is no official equivalence table between ISCED and EQF levels, a loose correspondence exists: a qualification at a higher EQF level is likely to correspond to a programme provided at a higher ISCED level (European Commission, 2008[20]). Drawing on a recent overview of national VET systems in Europe by Cedefop, Table 1.1 sets out how programmes in different countries are situated on the ISCED and the EQF framework respectively. While higher ISCED levels are associated with higher EQF levels, there is variation across countries and programmes in which EQF level is associated with a particular ISCED level. For example, in Poland some five-year upper secondary vocational programmes (ISCED 3) lead to an EQF 4 qualification, while 3-year sectoral programmes (also ISCED 3) lead to a EQF 3 qualification. ISCED 5 business academy programmes in Denmark lead to EQF 5 qualifications, while in the Czech Republic performing arts programmes (also ISCED 5) lead to EQF 6 qualifications.

Table 1.1. The position of vocational or professional programmes in European countries

ISCED level of the programme	EQF level attributed to the qualification
2	1, 2, 3
3	2, 3, 4
4	4, 5
5	5, 6
6	5, 6
7	7
8	8

Source: Synthesis based on information provided in Cedefop (2021[21]), *Spotlight on VET - 2020 compilation: vocational education and training systems in Europe*, http://data.europa.eu/10.2801/10.2801/667443; European Commission (2008[20]), *Explaining the European Qualifications Framework for Lifelong Learning*, https://europa.eu/europass/system/files/2020-05/EQF-Archives-EN.pdf.

This report draws on several sources of comparative data, most of which build on the ISCED 2011 framework (see Table 1.2 for an overview). Some allow for a breakdown by programme orientation at several tertiary levels, in line with the detailed ISCED classification (i.e. the Unesco-OECD-Eurostat [UOE] and LSO data collections, and the "Data collection on professional tertiary education"). In addition, data sources that do not allow for such a breakdown can provide useful insights in two ways. First, some sources (e.g. European Union Labour Force Survey [EU-LFS]) allow for the identification of ISCED 5 programmes, which are predominantly professional (see below). Second, some sources (e.g. EU-LFS, "Ad hoc survey on tertiary completion") provide insights on the pathways pursued by graduates of upper secondary VET, in particular their entry and progression through tertiary education. Given that in some countries professional tertiary programmes are extensively used by upper secondary VET graduates, this analysis provides insights that are relevant for professional programmes in those countries. All data sources are based on surveys, with the exception of the UOE data collection, which draws on administrative data.

Table 1.2. Sources of comparative data on professional tertiary education

Data source	Availability of data by orientation	How are data used?
UOE, LSO regular data collections	Yes, based on ISCED 2011	Professional programmes identified as all ISCED 5 programmes and ISCED 6 programmes currently reported as professional. Issues in focus: entry, enrolment, graduation, attainment and labour market outcomes in professional programmes.
Ad hoc survey on tertiary completion	No (only for prior upper secondary qualification)	Focus on ISCED 6 students with a vocational background, recognising the common use of professional programmes as a learning pathway for VET graduates. Issues in focus: share of students with a vocational background, completion rates.
Data collection on professional tertiary education	Yes, based on ISCED 2011	Professional programmes identified as all ISCED 5 programmes and ISCED 6 programmes currently reported as professional. Issues in focus: programme characteristics, data availability.
EU-LFS	No	Professional programmes identified as all ISCED 5 programmes. Issues in focus: progression patterns between levels of education, participation in work-based learning and employment outcomes.[2]
Survey of Adult Skills (PIAAC)	Yes, based on ISCED 97	Only ISCED 5B programmes can be identified, which correspond loosely to ISCED 5 programmes under the ISCED 2011 framework. Issues in focus: literacy and numeracy skills, links between field-of-study and subsequent occupation.

Most data from the UOE and LSO regular data collections were collected for *Education at a Glance 2020*, the latest data collection available for this project. The "Ad hoc survey on tertiary completion" was carried out for *Education at a Glance 2019* and data are used in this report to analyse the progression of VET graduates in tertiary education (ISCED 6 only). The "OECD Data collection on professional tertiary education" was conducted for this project in 2021, to understand what is currently reported as professional, identify the possibilities and constraints countries face when reporting data, as well as providing qualitative information on professional programmes.

In addition, the analysis draws on data from the European Union Labour Force Survey (EU-LFS) and the Survey of Adult Skills, a product of the Programme for the International Assessment of Adult Competencies (PIAAC), .These sources do not allow for a breakdown by orientation, but allow for the identification of ISCED 5 programmes and ISCED 5B programmes respectively. EU-LFS data are used to analyse the progression of VET graduates into tertiary education, while the Survey of Adult Skills (PIAAC) provides insights into outcomes from tertiary education.

Box 1.4 sets out how this report uses different terms to refer to the orientation of tertiary programmes.

> **Box 1.4. Terminology used in this report**
>
> This report uses the term **professional** to refer to all programmes at ISCED level 5, regardless of their current classification in international data collections. For ISCED levels 6 and 7, this report refers to programmes as "professional" (or "academic" or having "unspecified orientation") based on how they are classified in ISCED mappings and related international data collections. The terms **sector-oriented** and **profession-oriented** are used in this report as described in the proposals for internationally agreed definitions in this chapter.
>
> This report refers to professional tertiary programmes, as this term is used in the current ISCED framework. Other commonly used terms exist – **higher VET** in particular is often used, especially across Europe to refer to postsecondary and tertiary programmes with professional orientation. The definitions proposed in this chapter for sector-oriented and profession-oriented programmes is consistent with the broad definition of higher VET proposed by a recent European study (Ulicna, Luomi Messerer and Auzinger, 2016[8]), as they also include programmes covered by the European Higher Education Area. Finally, the terms **professionally-oriented** and **applied** are used in this report when used in the relevant context by the countries concerned (e.g. universities of applied sciences, professionally-oriented degrees).

Short-cycle tertiary qualifications – ISCED level 5

The availability of comparative data

Both country coverage and comparability of data at ISCED level 5 are good. Data collections for "professional" programmes at this level are based on the internationally agreed definitions of 'vocational'. Across OECD countries, the vast majority of students enrolled at level 5 pursue programmes classified as professional (Figure 1.4). Many of the remaining programmes appear to be professional despite being classified otherwise. For example, in the United Kingdom a recent mapping of the ISCED 5 landscape found it was mostly professional (Boniface, Whalley and Goodwin, 2018[22]) and programmes classified as "academic" include for example, training for paramedics, nurses and social workers. The classification choice is based on the provider institution, so that all programmes delivered in universities are reported as "academic". Similarly, in Iceland one of the two programmes in the academic category is called "short practical programme". Three countries report all students at this level in programmes with "unspecified orientation". In Ireland this level is composed of higher certificates, which appear to have a professional focus – they are offered in fields like accounting, business and property management (Courses.ie, 2021[23]). Similarly, in Costa Rica the two programmes reported at this level are "higher technical education" and teacher training. The United States is an exception in the sense that associate degrees include a mix: around 40% of associate degrees are conferred in the field of liberal arts and sciences, general studies and humanities (e.g. mathematics, geography), while the remaining 60% are within applied fields (e.g. business, health professions, engineering) (NCES, 2021[24]). The considerable share of qualifications in non-professional fields might be explained by the fact that in the United States associate degrees are commonly used as a stepping stone into bachelor's programmes (see Box 2.1 in Chapter 2).

Figure 1.4. Distribution of students by programme orientation at short-cycle tertiary level (2018)

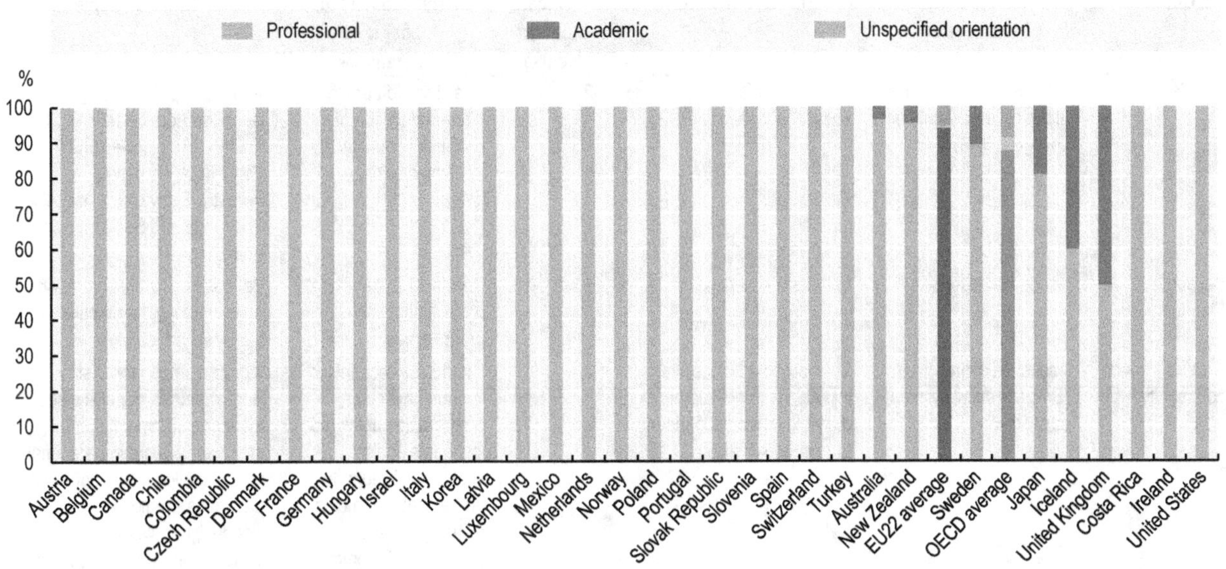

Note: Data are based on national definitions of programme orientation.
Source: OECD (2021[25]), "Education at a Glance", Education and Training – Education at a Glance (database), https://stats.oecd.org/.

StatLink https://stat.link/ivqmg3

Recognising that the vast majority of ISCED 5 students are in programmes that are professional at least in some sense, this report treats all programmes at this level as professional, regardless of their current classification. This approach has two advantages. It allows data by tertiary level to be compared meaningfully even when a breakdown by orientation is not possible. In addition, it broadens the country coverage of the analysis to include Costa Rica, Ireland and the United States. Given this approach, there is no impact in the 25 countries where all students are reported in professional programmes. In the remaining nine countries this approach may overestimate professional enrolment (in particular in those where a non-negligible proportion of the level 5 programmes appear to be non-professional, as in the United States). The internationally agreed definition for vocational programme orientation is used by countries in their data reporting, but the term "professional" is used in our analysis for simplicity and in line with the ISCED 2011 recommendation to use the term "professional" for all levels of tertiary education.

Common types of qualifications covered by comparative data

Associate degrees and short higher vocational programmes

Short-cycle tertiary qualifications are very often two years full-time, with options for articulation into bachelor's degrees at the same institution (or the same type of institution) and a considerable share of graduates pursue higher level studies (see Chapter 2 on pathways). Across countries, this category includes associate degrees taught in universities of applied science in Belgium-Flanders, associate degrees (BES qualifications) in the French Community of Belgium, Higher National Qualifications in Scotland (United Kingdom), foundation degrees in England (United Kingdom) and college diplomas in Canada (see Table 1.3). Some programmes are closely connected to upper secondary education and are provided within the same institutions as upper secondary VET programmes – examples include Austrian BHS programmes in which the programme (years 4 and 5) follow-up on three-year upper-secondary programmes in the same colleges.

Table 1.3. Short-cycle tertiary qualifications

Country	Programme / qualification	Provider institution	Typical duration (years)	Articulation with higher level programmes	Targeted fields
Austria	Grades 4-5 in (higher technical and vocational colleges (BHS)	Higher technical and vocational colleges (BHS)	2	Possibility to pursue higher education at a university or university of applied science.	Various (e.g. Technology, Business Administration, Fashion, Artistic Design, Tourism, Agriculture and Forestry, Early Childhood Pedagogy and Social Pedagogy)
Belgium-Flanders	Associate degree	University colleges	1.5-2	Possibility to transfer to professional bachelor's programmes.	Various (e.g. architecture, arts, biotechnology, healthcare, business, education)
Belgium-French community	Associate degree (Brevet d'enseignement supérieur)	Specialised adult learning institutions (établissements d'enseignement supérieur de promotion sociale)	2	Credits are recognised in short bachelor's programmes delivered in 'hautes écoles', écoles supérieurs des arts et établissements d'enseignement supérieur de promotion sociale.	9 programmes proposed : literacy trainer, general stage manager, commercial unit manager, advisor in personnel administration & management, tour guide - regional guide, webdesigner, webdeveloper, socio-professional integration advisor, animator in collective political, cultural & social action.
Canada	Undergraduate diploma/certificate; college diploma; advanced/applied certificate or diploma; post certificate or diploma; AVS	Various (e.g. public colleges, specialized institutes, community colleges, institutes of technology and advanced learning, and CÉGEPs)	1-3		Various (e.g. business, health, science, agriculture, applied arts, technology, skilled trades, and social services)
Chile	Higher technician	Professional training centres, Professional institutes	m.	Possibility to progress to 4-year programmes offered within the same institution.	m.
Czech Republic	Conservatoire programmes	Conservatoire	2	m.	Performing arts (music, singing, drama).
Denmark	Business academy programmes	Business academies	2	In some programmes students have the option of pursuing a top-up degree of 1.5 years to obtain a professional bachelor's degree.	Wide range of fields (e.g. automotive technology; design, technology and business; computer science; and various areas of management (logistics, marketing, service, hospitality and tourism).
France	Brevet de technicien supérieur (BTS)	Vocational upper secondary school or higher institute.	2	m.	m.
Israel	Initial training for technicians and practical engineers, job training programmes.	High schools, vocational training centres, colleges for practical engineers	m.	m.	m.
Italy	Professional tertiary education	Higher technical institutes	2-3	m.	6 technological areas: Energy efficiency, Sustainable mobility, New technologies for life, New technologies for "Made in Italy", Information and communication technologies, Innovative technologies for cultural heritage and activities - Tourism
Korea	Junior college course	Junior colleges	m.	m.	m.

Country	Programme / qualification	Provider institution	Typical duration (years)	Articulation with higher level programmes	Targeted fields
Latvia	Short-cycle higher education	Colleges	m.	m.	m.
Luxembourg	Brevet de technicien supérieur (BTS)	High schools	2	m.	Applied arts, trade, industry, health, services, wood technology.
Luxembourg	Continuing education for existing professionals	Universities	m.	m.	m.
Netherlands	Associate degree	Universities of applied sciences	2	m.	Business & management, technology, education, IT, care and welfare etc.
Norway	Vocational college programmes	Vocational colleges	2	Upon completion, students with a vocational upper secondary qualification gain access to universities and university colleges.	Programmes prepare master craftsmen, skilled technicians or para-professional occupations. Most students are graduates of upper secondary VET in technical fields, health or welfare.
Portugal	Vocational and technical higher education courses (CteSP)	Polytechnics	2	Articulation with bachelor's programmes.	Digital technology and arts, IT, Technology, Management, Art, communication and culture.
Slovenia	Short-cycle higher VET	Higher vocational colleges (most are part of upper secondary school centres)	2	m.	32 target professions
Spain	Higher vocational programmes leading to 'higher technician' qualifications.	m.	2 (3 if dual training)	m.	Various (e.g. Healthcare, Management, Hospitality, Electronics, Arts and design, ICT).
Sweden	Advanced diploma in higher VET	Different providers, mostly private organisations	2	m.	m.
United Kingdom	Higher National Certificate	Colleges, training providers, some universities	1	Possibility to enter into the second year of a degree programme	Wide range of subjects, e.g. business administration, computing, engineering, health and social care, social sciences.
United Kingdom	Higher National Diploma	Colleges, training providers, some universities	2	Possibility to enter into the third year of a degree programme	Wide range of subjects, e.g. business administration, computing, engineering, health and social care, social sciences.

Note: The list of qualifications is not exhaustive, additional qualifications may exist in some countries. m.= missing
Source: OECD Data collection on professional tertiary education.

Professional examinations

Some ISCED 5 qualifications are delivered following a professional examination. Box 1.5 describes the general approach of professional examinations, which exist in several OECD countries and yield qualifications at several tertiary levels depending on the country and target occupation. At ISCED 5, Austria has examinations following preparation in a *Meisterschule*. In Germany *meister* examinations that follow a short preparatory programme lead to level 5 qualifications and the title "Certified occupational specialist", and are available in a range of target occupations (e.g. opticians, plumbers and heating engineers).

> **Box 1.5. Professional examinations: Advanced qualifications based on an examination**
>
> Professional examinations exist in some form in several OECD countries. They are designed to upskill those already working in a profession, typically with an earlier vocational qualification in the field. One of their key characteristics is that they do not require any specific programme of preparation, although having several years of relevant work experience is a common requirement. In several countries such examinations are led by industry at the national level, leading to a qualification that is standardised and unique at national level. These qualifications and the (often optional and unregulated) programmes that prepare candidates are reported in ISCED mappings and captured by comparative data. They lead to qualifications at ISCED levels 5, 6 and 7 depending on the country and the target occupation. Examinations have traditionally led to *meister* qualifications for traditional VET occupations, preparing for example qualified electricians and plumbers to run their own business and train apprentices. Mirroring developments within the VET system, qualifications have diversified in terms of targeted sectors and are now available in sectors like healthcare, IT and finance.
>
> **Germany**: Professional examinations are a common entryway to higher professional and management positions. An initial vocational qualification within the same or related field is a prerequisite, but it may be replaced by several years of relevant work experience. They exist at three levels: short programmes (less than 880 hours of preparatory coursework) yield the title "Certified occupational specialist" (ISCED level 5), longer master craftsmen programmes yield the title "Bachelor Professional" (ISCED level 6). In addition ISCED level 7 examinations were introduced recently and lead to the title Master professional.
>
> **Switzerland**: Federal professional examinations lead to a Federal Diploma of Higher Education (ISCED level 6) or Advanced Federal Diploma of Higher Education (ISCED level 7). They are intended for professionals who have completed upper secondary VET and seek to improve their knowledge and skills, or develop specialised skills. Candidates may pursue preparatory courses for the examinations and they typically do so while continuing to work in the corresponding field. The courses are not regulated, as they are optional. Providers of such courses include local authorities, professional organisations, individual or groups of companies, and private education providers.
>
> Source: Kis and Windisch (2018[26]), "*Making skills transparent: Recognising vocational skills acquired through workbased learning*", OECD Education Working Papers, No. 180, https://doi.org/10.1787/5830c400-en; OECD Data collection on professional tertiary education; Gewerbeanmeldung.de (2022[27]), *Informationen zur Gewerbeanmeldung* [Information on business registration], www.gewerbeanmeldung.de/meisterpflicht; SDBB (2022[28]), *Das offizielle schweizerische Informationsportal der Berufs-, Studien- und Laufbahnberatung (Le portail officiel suisse d'information de l'orientation professionnelle, universitaire et de carrière)*, https://www.berufsberatung.ch/.

Programmes delivered outside formal education and training are excluded

In some countries, preparatory courses for professional examinations are excluded. In Austria, for example, preparatory courses outside formal education are not captured by enrolment and graduation data. More broadly, in most countries industry-led certifications, which lead to similar qualifications to professional examinations but without public involvement, are excluded from comparative data collections.

Bachelor's level qualifications – ISCED level 6

The availability of comparative data

Comparative data on professional programmes at level 6 are available for 15 countries, based on national definitions of programme orientation. About half of OECD countries do not distinguish programmes by orientation at ISCED level 6 and four countries report all of their students in academic programmes. Two reasons are likely to explain this. First, some countries may find the professional-academic distinction less relevant to their system or difficult to implement because they have a unified tertiary system without distinct institutional or programme categories. Second, some countries may prefer not to report a distinction that is possibly ambiguous given the absence of internationally agreed definitions. Among the 15 countries that choose to report professional programmes at this level, some of the variation in the distribution of students is driven by different classification choices for similar programmes (as discussed above, see Figure 1.5).

Figure 1.5. Distribution of students by programme orientation at bachelor's or equivalent level (2018)

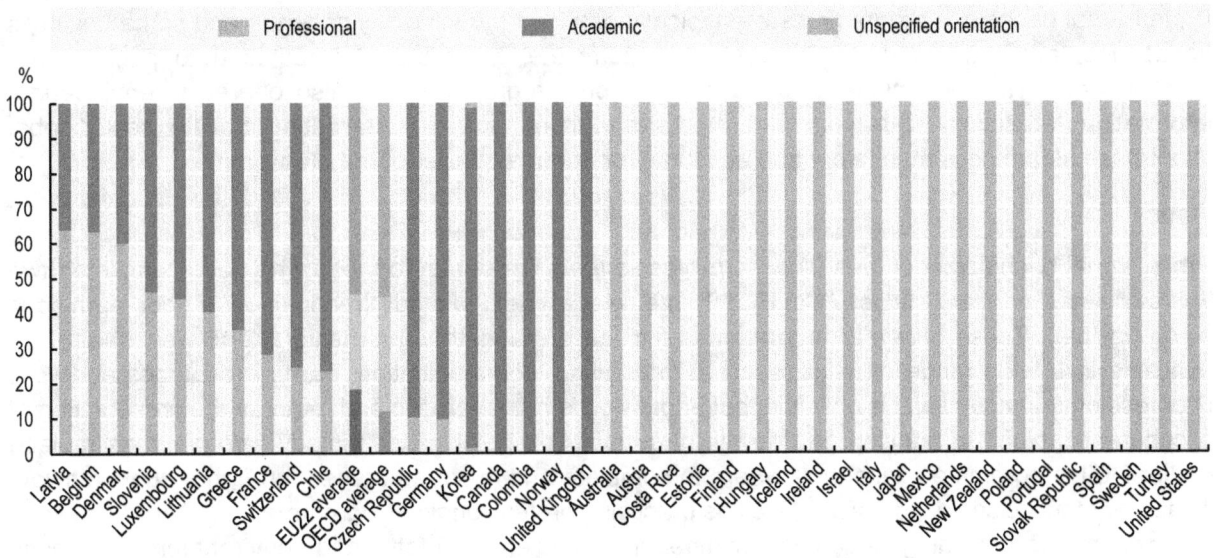

Note: Data are based on national definitions of programme orientation.
Source: OECD (2021[9]), "Education at a Glance", Education and Training – Education at a Glance (database), https://stats.oecd.org/.

StatLink https://stat.link/vuexd4

Common types of qualifications covered by comparative data

Professional bachelor's programmes

Professional bachelor's programmes, involving professional training through a bachelor's degree, are increasingly common in Europe (see Box 1.6). They are often taught in dedicated institutions, such as universities of applied sciences or university colleges. They have seen rapid growth in several countries, where enrolment now rivals or exceeds the level of academic bachelor's degrees (e.g. Belgium, the Netherlands). While some programmes prepare for a single occupation (e.g. nurse, teacher), many take as their point of departure the applications of a particular type of science – for example food technology or business management. This means that they provide the knowledge and skills associated with a family of professions or a particular sector, linked to the application of that type of science.

> **Box 1.6. Professional bachelor's programmes**
>
> **Belgium-Flanders**
>
> Professional bachelor's programmes are only provided by university colleges and are oriented towards professional practice. They provide knowledge and competences required to pursue a profession or a group of professions. Graduates are prepared for immediate labour market entry. A "bachelor after bachelor" course is available as a follow-up to deepen expertise in specific areas. Progression to master level is possible after a bridging programme.
>
> **Denmark**
>
> Professional bachelor's programmes are typically provided by university colleges and some business academies, and take three or four years to complete. Most programmes lead to public-sector employment as teacher, nurse or social worker, but programmes are also offered in engineering, information technology, business and media and communication, targeting private sector jobs. Work-based learning is mandatory and accounts for about a quarter of the programme.
>
> **France**
>
> Professional bachelor's degrees (*license professionnelle*) are open to those who have completed two years of postsecondary studies (120 ECTS) in a relevant field of study (recognition of prior learning is also possible). These one-year programmes include a mandatory internship (12-16 weeks) and are available in a wide range of fields, such as marketing, communication, human resources and ICT. Progression to master level is possible, but admission is not automatic and requires the presentation of a coherent project. In addition, the newly introduced "bachelor of technology" programmes replace earlier DUT programmes, take three years to complete and may be pursued through a dual pathway. Teaching staff include academics as well as practicing professionals. Programmes on offer are diverse, with examples including industrial engineering, hygiene, safety and environment, business management, social careers, multimedia and Internet professions.
>
> **Latvia**
>
> Professional bachelor's programmes may be delivered by universities or university colleges. Their content must be designed according to approved professional standards established at national level. These standards are developed by expert groups, including employers and experts in the relevant field. Fields of study include management and administration, teacher training, ICT, travel, tourism and leisure, elderly care, social work and engineering trades. All programmes include a mandatory internship or one semester of practice.
>
> **Lithuania**
>
> Professional bachelor's degrees are oriented towards preparation for professional activity and applied research. They are delivered by colleges of higher education. Professional bachelor's degrees were introduced in 2007 and replaced Diplomas of Higher Education, which used to indicate the title of the awarded qualification (e.g. physiotherapist, educator) but were not degrees.

Slovenia

Professional first cycle study programmes provide students with the skills and expertise to apply scientific methods to the resolution of complex professional problems. Practical training in a working environment is mandatory. These study programs are based on legislation designed to implement reforms linked to the Bologna process. They take three to four years to complete and consist of 180 to 240 ECTS, similarly to academic first cycle programmes. They may be offered by universities, academies or professional colleges.

Source: MHES (2021[29]), *About the university colleges*, https://ufm.dk/en/education/higher-education/university-colleges/about-the-university-colleges; OECD Data collection on professional tertiary education; Orientation (2021[30]), *Les Bachelors Universitaires de Technologie (BUT) : Guide complet !*, https://www.orientation.com/diplomes/diplome-but.

Professional examinations

Professional examinations (see key principles in Box 1.5) are available at ISCED level 6 in a few countries. Box 1.7 provides some examples targeted professions. In Germany examinations at this level cover a range of fields, with bachelor professional titles available for example in procurement, bookkeeping, media, print, event technology. In Switzerland, most professional examinations are situated at ISCED level 6.

Box 1.7. Examples of professional examinations at ISCED level 6

Germany

Mechatronics meisters co-ordinate ongoing operations, control work processes, manage employees and train apprentices. The preparatory course provides technical knowledge to prepare candidates to take up responsibilities in the planning, optimisation and management of the manufacturing process. The course takes about two years to complete (full-time equivalent four months) and may be followed online, part-time on Saturdays, or full-time during the week.

Certified accountants create, analyse and interpret monthly, quarterly and annual reports and inform management decisions. Admission requires a relevant prior qualification and professional experience. Candidates with over five years of relevant work experience need no prior qualification. The preparatory course is taught by professionals from companies, management consultancies and combine both theoretical knowledge and practice-oriented content. The course takes about two years to complete when pursued parallel to employment and may be pursued in the evenings and weekends.

Switzerland

Audioprothesists adapt hearing aids to the needs of people with hearing impairment, based on the analysis of their medical files and their needs. They choose and adjust the hearing aid and pursue a long-term follow-up of patients (e.g. adjusting the settings of hearing aids, repairing). The preparatory course is composed of two modules of 18 months. Candidates must hold a vocational qualification or upper secondary school certificate and at least three years of professional experience.

> **International trade experts** perform administrative tasks related to the import/export of goods and services. They prepare documents that support a commercial transaction (e.g. credit, insurance and transport arrangements), negotiate the sales conditions (e.g. contracts, timing) and ensure that the financial risks related to new or risky clients are covered. The preparatory course takes around 19 months to complete. Candidates must hold a vocational qualification or upper secondary school certificate and at least two years of professional experience with an emphasis on international trade.
>
> Source: FAIN (2021[31]), *Industriemeister Mechatronik IHK – Jetzt IHK-geprüften Meistertitel machen – FAIN* [Master tradesperson in the mechatronics industry IHK – Get your IHK-certified master craftsperson title now – FAIN], https://www.fain.de/angebote/industriemeister-mechatronik-ihk; DIHK (2022[32]), *Bilanzbuchhalter – Bachelor Professional in Bilanzbuchhaltung* [Accountant – Bachler Professional in Balance Sheet Accounting], https://www.dihk-bildungs-gmbh.de/weiterbildung/top-weiterbildungsabschluesse/bilanzbuchhalter; SDBB (2022[28]), *Das offizielle schweizerische Informationsportal der Berufs-, Studien- und Laufbahnberatung (Le portail officiel suisse d'information de l'orientation professionnelle, universitaire et de carrière)*, https://www.berufsberatung.ch/.

In some countries applied bachelor's programmes are not classified as professional

In various countries, bachelor's programmes with similarly applied, occupationally-oriented focus are not classified as professional in international data collections. For example, Austria, Germany and Switzerland currently report programmes delivered in universities of applied sciences as academic, while Finland and the Netherlands report them as having "unspecified orientation". While there are differences in the precise role and nature of UASs in different countries, the descriptions of these institutions suggest they share a number of features with UASs that deliver programmes currently classified as professional. For example, in Austria, the UASs describe programmes as "professionally oriented", with 3-year bachelor's programmes offered in fields like Business, Engineering and IT, Social Sciences, Media and Design, Health Sciences (OEAD, 2019[33]). In Germany, the UAS are described as providing academic studies with a practical focus and an "orientation towards vocational requirements" (DAAD, 2021[34]). Switzerland describes its universities of applied science as offering "practice-oriented and application-oriented degree programmes which lead to professional qualifications". Similarly, in Finland the UAS sector has "the mission to train professionals with emphasis on labour market needs" (studyinfo.fi, 2021[35]) and in the Netherlands UASs focus on the "practical application of arts and sciences" (Study in Holland, 2021[36])and train for a specific profession (TU Delft, 2021[37]). Box 1.8 describes the UAS sector in the Netherlands, which has grown rapidly over the past decades and now enrols more students at bachelor's level than regular universities.

> **Box 1.8. Universities of applied sciences in the Netherlands**
>
> The Netherlands has a binary system of higher education, with 13 academic universities and 41 universities of applied sciences or *hoger beroepsonderwijs* (HBO) institutions. Following the implementation of the Bologna process, academic universities reorganised their offer of earlier four-year programmes into three-year academic bachelor's programmes typically followed by one or two-year master's degrees. Programmes provided by UASs remained unchanged in duration but were designated as professional bachelor's degrees (Allen and Belfi, 2020[38]).
>
> Both types of institutions offer programmes in a wide range of fields with many overlaps but differences in terms of focus. While academic universities focus on research, UAS programmes focus on the practical application of arts and sciences (Study in Holland, 2021[36])For example, Delft University of Technology describes UAS programmes as training for a specific profession while academic programmes focus on an analytical and critical approach to particular disciplines. UAS programmes are designed to apply and improve existing knowledge and involve practice-oriented assignments (TU Delft, 2021[37]).

> UASs have played an important role in the expansion of higher education. While academic universities may be accessed only upon completion of the highest upper secondary track, UASs are accessible for completers of other tracks as well (i.e. either *HAVO* or the highest tier of classroom-based or workplace-based vocational training) (Allen and Belfi, 2020[38]).
>
> Source: Allen and Belfi (2020[38]), "Educational expansion in the Netherlands: better chances for all?", *Oxford Review of Education*, Vol. 46/1, pp. 44-62, https://doi.org/10.1080/03054985.2019.1687435; Study in Holland (2021[36]), *Universities of applied sciences*, https://www.studyinholland.nl/dutch-education/universities-of-applied-sciences; TU Delft (2021[37]), *What's the difference between HBO and WO?*, https://www.tudelft.nl/en/education/information-and-experience/preparing-for-a-bachelor/whats-the-difference-between-hbo-and-wo#c244116.

Some newly introduced programmes are also excluded from the comparative data currently available for this report. Italy introduced experimental bachelor's degrees with professional orientation in 2018. Designed to facilitate entry into the world of work, professionally-oriented degree courses must build on agreements with companies or professional associations, include an internship and ensure that 60% of graduates are employed within one year of graduation. Following the experimental stage, new professionally-oriented degree courses were introduced in 2020 in construction and the territory, agricultural, food and forestry technical professions, and industrial and ICT technical professions (OECD, 2021[25]).

Finally, in countries with 'unified' higher education systems, including many English-speaking countries, the kinds of programmes offered in universities of applied science are delivered in multi-purpose higher education institutions (universities or colleges). These are nearly always classified as having "unspecified orientation" in comparative data.

Master's level qualifications – ISCED level 7

The availability of comparative data

Comparative data on professional programmes at level 7 are only available for 12 countries, and are based on national definitions of programme orientation (see Figure 1.6). Most other countries report all students under unspecified programme orientation and some consider all programmes at this level as academic. As for ISCED level 6, in the absence of internationally agreed definitions, different classification choices inevitably drive much of the variation in enrolment numbers. For example, in France, the high share of professional students at master's level reflects how many programmes are classified as professional: engineering, business, law, accountability, education, medicine, pharmacy, odontology and midwifery. Most other countries treat such advanced programmes, including for medical professions and engineers, as academic or unspecified.

In summary, given comparative data limited to 12 countries, the lack of definitions to underpin comparability, and the lesser quantitative role of ISCED level 7 relative to levels 5 and 6, subsequent chapters of this report will exclude ISCED level 7.

Figure 1.6. Distribution of students by programme orientation at master's or equivalent level (2018)

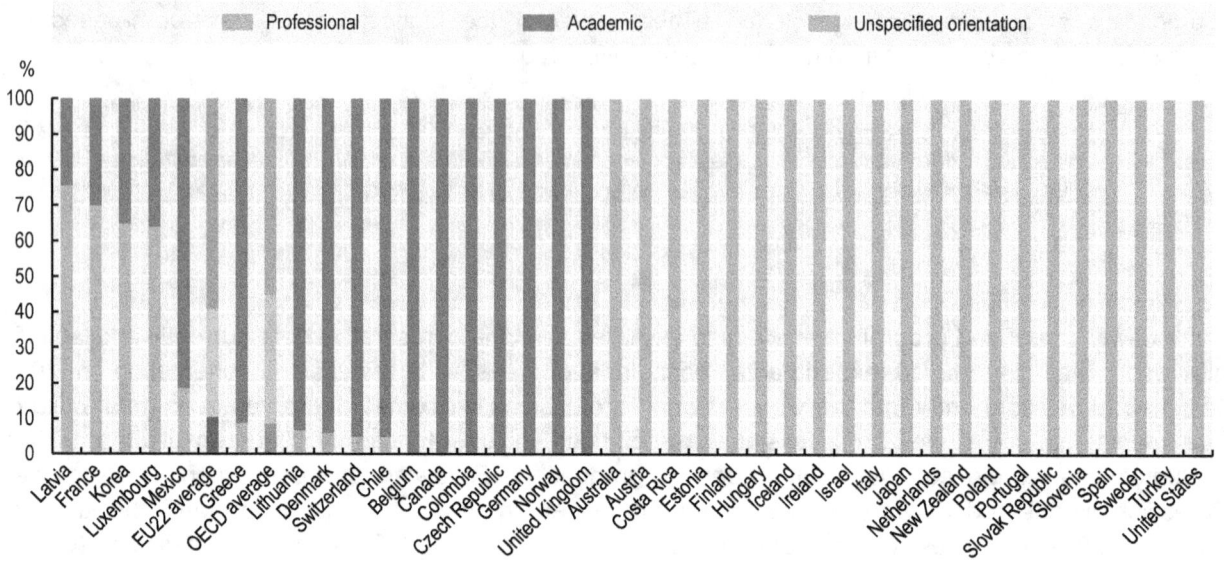

Note: Data are based on national definitions of programme orientation.
Source: OECD (2021[9]), "Education at a Glance", Education and Training – Education at a Glance (database), https://stats.oecd.org/.

StatLink https://stat.link/ro6uxh

Common types of qualifications covered by comparative data

Professional master's and advanced specialisation programmes

Professional master's degrees exist in the Netherlands (see Box 1.9), where they are offered in universities of applied science. They cover a wide range of fields and offer a higher learning opportunity to graduates of professional bachelor's programmes. Other advanced specialisation programmes reported as professional typically take one or two years to complete. These include programmes in the field of healthcare, such as medical or dental graduate specialisation programmes in Chile, medical residency in Lithuania, professional training for general practitioners in Luxembourg and post-degree specialist health studies in Spain. Some teacher training programmes are included in this category in France, Israel and Luxembourg. In Luxembourg programmes preparing for an examination for chartered accountants or chartered auditors is included.

Box 1.9. Professional master's degrees in the Netherlands

Programmes are available in a wide range of fields, such as education (e.g. qualifications for teachers or school leaders), economy and business (e.g. MBA, customer management, finance and control), healthcare (e.g. advanced nursing, medical imaging), art and culture (e.g. interior architecture, music). Programmes differ from university master's degrees in that they have a stronger professional orientation and less emphasis on research and analytical skills. Professional master's programmes offer an upskilling option for graduates of professional bachelor's programmes, as direct access is possible (while master's degrees offered at universities are only accessible to them after a bridging course).

Source: StudieKeuze123.nl (2022[39]), *Objectieve informatie over alle erkende hbo- en wo-opleidingen van Nederland* [Objective information about all recognised university and university of applied sciences programmes in the Netherlands], https://www.studiekeuze123.nl/.

Professional examinations

A few countries have professional examinations at ISCED level 7 (see Box 1.5 on professional examinations in general and Box 1.10 for specific examples). In Switzerland, this qualification is wellestablished offering advanced specialisation to professionals who have acquired a great deal of expertise in their field and/or who intend to hold a managerial position in a company. In Germany the title "Master Professional" was introduced in 2020 to refer to advanced professional qualifications. In Luxembourg, programmes with similar features are run by universities. For example, programmes preparing for the examination for chartered accountants or chartered auditors in Luxembourg is taught in two semesters, combined with work-based learning.

> **Box 1.10. Examples of professional examinations at ISCED level 7**
>
> **Financial analyst and wealth manager - Switzerland**
>
> Financial analysts and wealth managers study companies that are typically listed on the stock exchange. They assess the financial instruments issues by companies (e.g. stocks, bonds) and develop investment strategies and manage portfolios, based on careful consideration of the interests of the clients and those of the institution. Financial analysts focus mostly on providing information and advice, while wealth managers focus on investments.
>
> Candidates must hold a vocational or general upper secondary school certificate plus at least five years of experience in banking or finance (or higher level studies with fewer years of experience, e.g. a bachelor's degree or federal diploma of higher education plus three years of relevant experience). The examination consists of three modules: Financial accounting and analysis, equity, corporate finance and economics; Fixed income, derivatives and portfolio management; the Swiss market, ethics, law and taxation.
>
> **Technical management – Germany**
>
> The programme is delivered online through seminars and webinars and takes about 12 months to complete part time, while participants are employed (classes take place in the evening with live webinars every week). The full-time version of the course takes 11 weeks to complete. Targeted preparation for the examination is offered to both part-time and full-time students. The examination is conducted by local industrial and commercial chamber. The written part of the examination is common across all chambers in Germany.
>
> **Chartered accountants – Luxembourg**
>
> The University of Luxembourg offers a two-semester programme preparing for examinations for chartered accountants. Courses are taught in 3-4 hour blocks, three days a week. Candidates will be considered for the examination only if they are pursuing an internship approved by relevant financial control authorities or with a chartered accountant.
>
> Source: manQ e.K. (2022[40]), *Master Professional - Technischer Betriebswirt (IHK)* [Master Professional – Technical Business Administration (IHK)], https://www.management-qualifizierung.de/kursangebote/betriebswirte/technischer-betriebswirt-ihk; SDBB (2022[28]), *Das offizielle schweizerische Informationsportal der Berufs-, Studien- und Laufbahnberatung (Le portail officiel suisse d'information de l'orientation professionnelle, universitaire et de carrière)*, https://www.berufsberatung.ch/; Université de Luxembourg (2022[41]), *Formation complémentaire des candidats réviseurs d'entreprises et experts-comptables*, https://wwwfr.uni.lu/formations/fdef/formation_complementaire_des_candidats_reviseurs_d_entreprises_et_experts_comptables.

Long first degrees

Some programmes reported by countries in this category are "long first degrees", which require at least five years to compete, may be started directly after upper secondary education and lead to a qualification that is equivalent to a master's degree. These are often five or six year programmes in medical fields, law or engineering. For example, France applies a broad definition of "professional" and includes five-year business schools and long first degree programmes in law, medicine, pharmacy and odontology in this category. The Czech Republic reports career-oriented master's study programmes, which take five or six years to complete.

Comparative data capture a small part of programmes at this level

Programmes at ISCED level 7 that are similar to those described above as professional are classified as academic or unspecified in most OECD countries and are excluded from comparative data on professional programmes. For example, as shown in Figure 1.3, training for lawyers and medical doctors is treated as professional by only two out of 26 countries, while over 20 countries include these programmes in the category of academic or unspecified orientation. Similarly, advanced specialisation courses are treated as academic or unspecified by many countries – for example half of the countries that responded to our survey report training for accountants as having academic or unspecified orientation.

In addition, qualifications akin to advanced professional examinations in some countries are delivered outside the formal education and training system, and are therefore not covered by comparative data collections based on ISCED mappings. Box 1.11 describes the example of training for patent attorneys in the United Kingdom, which builds on an undergraduate qualification but only sometimes includes an element of formal education (the Foundation Certificate course).

Box 1.11. Training for patent attorneys in the United Kingdom

Patent attorneys assess whether inventions are new and innovative, and therefore eligible to be patented. They are typically employed by law firms, the law department of large industrial companies or government departments. It usually takes four to six years to qualify as a patent attorney. Candidates need a degree in a science, engineering, technical or mathematics-based subject. Training takes place on the job and includes self-directed study, in-house support and guidance, as well as external training courses. At foundation level, candidates must complete either an accredited Foundation Certificate examination or pursue an accredited Foundation Certificate course provided by a university. The subsequent final diploma examination tests candidates' knowledge of intellectual property law, skills in drafting and amending patent applications, and capacity to assess a patent's validity. In addition, candidates must undertake two years' of supervised full-time practice or at least four years of unsupervised full-time practice in intellectual property. Successful candidates become chartered patent attorneys.

Source: Prospects.ac.uk (2022[42]), *Job profile - Patent attorney*, https://www.prospects.ac.uk/job-profiles/patent-attorney.

The landscape of provider institutions

Table 1.4 provides an overview of the types of institutions that deliver short-cycle tertiary programmes (regardless of how their orientation is classified) and bachelor's programmes, distinguishing between academic and professional programmes in countries that choose to draw a distinction.

Several countries deliver short-cycle programmes in dedicated institutions, which do not provide programmes above ISCED 5. These are either specialised technical institutions (e.g. vocational colleges in Norway, colleges in Poland) or educational institutions that also deliver upper secondary programmes (e.g. technical and vocational colleges in Austria, vocational secondary schools in the Slovak Republic and vocational colleges in Slovenia). In some countries certain types of institutions can deliver only ISCED 5 qualifications, while other types of institutions may deliver programmes at ISCED level 5 and ISCED 6 (and above). For example, in Latvia colleges may offer only short-cycle tertiary education, while other higher education institutions may offer tertiary programmes at all levels.

Multi-level institutions with an applied, professional focus are common in Europe. These include universities of applied sciences, university colleges and colleges, which are distinct from regular universities. Such institutions have the common characteristic that they undertake research in applied fields and train students for various professions or sectors. However, programmes delivered in such institutions are classified differently in comparative data collections. For example, Belgium (Flanders), Denmark and Lithuania treat programmes taught in these institutions as professional in international data collections, while Germany, Norway and Switzerland consider them academic and Austria, Finland and the Netherlands report all programmes at ISCED level 6 and above under "unspecified orientation".

In some countries the kind of applied science programmes found in UAS-s or university colleges are found in ordinary universities. A recent European study (CEDEFOP, 2019[43]) identifies this approach as a 'unified' system, and in Europe, considers only Iceland and Spain, alongside the United Kingdom, in having such systems. England (UK) established polytechnic institutions in the 1970s with many of the same characteristics as the UAS-s, but subsequently merged polytechnics back into the university system from 1992 (Field, 2018[44]). Other countries maintain separate more professionally oriented systems of further and higher education, including TAFE institutions in Australia, and community colleges in the United States and Canada, but these systems much less often offer bachelor's degrees at ISCED level 6, and instead offer a diverse area of programmes, including two year programmes at ISCED level 5 that are intended to articulate into bachelor's programmes in universities, so they are not really comparable with UAS-s. In many English-speaking countries multi-purpose universities provide a full range of programmes at bachelor's level, including programmes that might be classified as general, sector- or profession-oriented.

Finally, the institutions delivering preparatory courses for professional examinations are subject to little regulation and include a wide range of providers (see Box 1.12).

Box 1.12. Preparatory courses for professional examinations in Switzerland

There is a great variety of institutions that provide preparatory courses for federal examinations. They include providers run by local authorities, professional organisations, individual or groups of companies. Some are private education providers, while some have a mixed public-private ownership. The preparatory courses themselves are not regulated, as they are optional. A major recent reform was the introduction of subsidies in 2018, which cover 50% of the tuition cost of preparatory courses. This reform aimed to put adults preparing for federal examinations on equal footing with students in PET colleges, UAS-s and academic universities, signalling that higher VET has equal value to university studies. Prior to the reform the only support available for those preparing for federal examinations was a contribution from their employer.

Source: OECD Data collection on professional tertiary education.

Table 1.4. Type of institutions delivering tertiary programmes

ISCED 5 and 6 programmes by level of education and orientation

| | Short-cycle tertiary | Bachelor | |
| | | Academic | Professional |
	(1)	(2)	(3)
OECD			
Australia	Some secondary education providers, vocational education providers, some universities.	Universities.	Universities and some vocational education providers.
Austria	Higher technical and vocational colleges, post-secondary colleges, technical and vocational schools, universities, other HEI-s	Universities, universities of applied sciences, university colleges of teacher education	n.a.
Belgium (Flanders)	Secondary education schools and university colleges	Universities	University colleges
Belgium (French Community)	Adult higher education	Universities, university colleges (high schools), adult higher education and higher arts schools	Universities, university colleges (high schools), adult higher education and higher arts schools
Canada	Colleges	Universities, colleges	
Chile	Technical training centres, professional institutes	Universities, professional institutes	Universities, professional institutes
Colombia	Universities, university institutions, professional technical institutions, technological institutions	Universities, university institutions	n.a.
Costa Rica	Universities, university institutions, professional technical institutions, technological institutions	Universities	
Czech Republic	Conservatoires	University and non-university HEI-s	University and non-university HEI-s, tertiary professional schools
Denmark	University colleges, business academies	Universities	Universities, university colleges, business academies, others
Estonia	m	Universities, professional HEI-s	
Finland	m	Universities, universities of applied science	
France	Universities, high schools, other institutions	Universities, high schools	Universities, private universities, specialised schools (e.g. Business, nursing, accountability)
Germany	Independent private training institutes, trade and technical schools	Universities, universities of applied science, cooperative state universities, colleges of public administration, vocational academies	Fachgymnasium, independent private training institutes, specialised vocational school, trade and technical school, vocational academies
Hungary	Universities	Universities, colleges	
Israel	Colleges	Universities, colleges	Universities, colleges
Italy	Higher level technical education institutions	Universities, specialised HEI-s (fine arts, drama, arts, music)	
Japan	Colleges of technology, junior colleges, specialised training colleges	Universities, colleges, colleges of technology, junior colleges, educational institutions other than universities that are recognized by NIAD-QE	
Korea	Colleges	Universities, colleges	Universities, colleges
Latvia	Universities, university colleges, colleges	Universities, university colleges	Universities, university colleges
Lithuania	n.a.	Universities	Colleges (small share in universities)
Luxembourg	Secondary schools	Universities	Universities

	Short-cycle tertiary	Bachelor	
		Academic	Professional
	(1)	(2)	(3)
Mexico	Technological universities, technological institutes	Universities, university colleges	n.a.
Netherlands	Universities of applied science (HBO)	Universities	Universities of applied science (HBO)
New Zealand	All HEI-s	All HEI-s	
Norway	Vocational colleges	Universities, university colleges	n.a.
Poland	Colleges	Universities, academies, non-university HEI-s	Universities, academies, non-university HEI-s
Portugal	Polytechnic institutions	Universities, polytechnic institutions	
Slovak Republic	Secondary vocational schools	Universities	
Slovenia	Vocational colleges	Universities, free-standing HEI-s	Universities, free-standing HEI-s
Spain	Universities, VET institutions	Universities	
Sweden	Universities, university colleges	Universities, university colleges	
Switzerland	Colleges of higher education, specialised providers of preparatory courses for federal examinations	Universities, universities of applied sciences, universities of teacher education	Colleges of higher education, specialised providers of preparatory courses for federal examinations
Turkey	Universities, non-profit foundation vocational schools	Universities	
United Kingdom	Further education providers, higher education providers	Higher education providers	n.a.
Partners			
Brazil	All types of HEI-s	All types of HEI-s	All types of HEI-s
EU non-OECD			
Cyprus	Institutes of tertiary education	Universities, institutes of tertiary education	

Note: n.a. not applicable; m missing information.
Source: OECD Data collection on professional tertiary education.

Towards internationally agreed definitions

Preliminary considerations

The professional-academic dichotomy is problematic

The etymology of "academic" relates to Plato's Academy of thinkers and philosophers, originally located outside Athens. "Academic" as an adjective in the English language, is derived from Latin and Middle French. Most dictionaries – for example Oxford Languages (Oxford Languages, 2020[45]), Cambridge, (Cambridge Dictionary, 2020[46]) – agree that "academic" as an adjective has two meanings. Definition 1 is relating to high level teaching, thinking and learning. The first identified use of the word in the 16th century is associated with this meaning. Definition 2 of "academic" is of no practical application: as when "a purely academic question" means that it is of no practical application or relevance. In this sense "academic" education is opposite, *by definition*, to practical, vocational or professional education and training.

These two meanings of "academic" are potentially contradictory, as high-level teaching, thinking and learning, obviously often *do* have practical applications. Previous research has already demonstrated that "vocational drift" and "academic drift" in institutional missions, rather than being substitutes, may take place simultaneously, with the academic-professional distinction being identified as "artificial" (CEDEFOP,

2019[43]). The meaning of "professional" is more straightforward, as in Oxford Languages "connected with a job that needs special training or skill, especially one that needs a high level of education". It is different from "vocational" in that definitions emphasise the high level of skills required.

"Academic" and "professional" are mutually exclusive categories if academic is used in the sense of definition 2, as all professional programmes have practical application and are therefore non-academic in that sense. However, this is unlikely to be widely acceptable. Institutions teaching law, medicine and universities of applied science are deeply attached to high-level teaching, thinking and learning – academic in the sense of definition 1, and are therefore not likely to be comfortable with their programmes being classified as non-academic simply because they involve applied, professional training.

Two major grey zones need to be addressed

Two groups of programme constitute major grey zones, as they tend to be categorised differently across countries. The first such grey zone concerns programmes that are both professional and academic (in the sense of definition 1). The current ISCED guidance treats academic and professional as mutually exclusive categories. Yet many programmes are professional in the sense that they prepare for a particular profession, and academic in the sense that they require high-level thinking and learning – it would be hard to argue that training for teachers and medical doctors is not academic simply because it prepares for the practice of a specific profession. Over 40% of young tertiary graduates (see Figure 4.1) benefitted from work-based learning during their tertiary studies, revealing close linkages between study programmes and the world of work. Faced with the difficult choice between academic *or* professional, in cases where both apply, countries make different choices in international reporting (see Figure 1.3). As a result, there is a high level of inconsistency across countries regarding the classification of these programmes.

The second grey zone includes programmes that are highly applied in nature but prepare students to work in a range of jobs in an occupational area or industry sector, rather than a single profession. For example, programmes in universities of applied science take as their point of departure the applications of a particular type of science, providing knowledge and skills associated with range of professions linked to that field. A bachelor's programme in food technology prepares individuals who are going to work in a range of roles (e.g. marketing, product development) in the food industry. In practice, such applied programmes have varying breadth and may have broad application (e.g. public management). Such programmes, in particular those provided in universities of applied science in Europe, are also classified very differently across countries. Universities of applied sciences (UAS) programmes are classified as "academic" in Germany and Switzerland, "professional" in Belgium (both French Community and Flanders) and as having "unspecified orientation" in Finland and the Netherlands.

Focusing on the professional dimension of programmes can add value

Recognising that "academic" in the sense of definition 1 and "professional" are not mutually exclusive, one option could be to develop a two-dimensional classification of programmes, but the next paragraphs argue that this would be neither desirable nor feasible. The "academic" dimension might measure how intellectually demanding programmes are in terms of higher level teaching, thinking and learning. The "professional" dimension might measure the extent to which the programme is applied in nature and designed to prepare for particular jobs. In theory, this could help with the classification of programmes in the grey zone, allowing for example programmes to be both highly "academic" and highly "professional" (e.g. advanced medical training) or have medium "academic" and medium "professional" content (e.g. business studies).

However, this would be problematic for both theoretical and practical reasons. ISCED levels already allow a classification of programmes taking into account their duration and complexity based on agreed guidance. Further disaggregation in terms of intellectual complexity would be problematic in relation to the EQF, according to which programmes at each EQF level have the same level of intellectual complexity. In addition, implementing this in practice would be extremely hard and would have limited added value for data collection and analysis. Operationalising distinctions of the degree of high-level thinking, teaching and learning for statistical purposes would be very difficult. For example, it would be extraordinarily difficult, in practice, to assess the competing claims for the level of "academic" content of programmes for accountants, computer scientists and history teachers, and any indicators arising from such appraisals would be of questionable value.

Therefore the proposal advanced in the following section is that only the "professional" dimension, i.e. the extent to which programmes prepare for a targeted (set of) occupation(s), should be used to classify the orientation of programmes (occupation is understood here as a particular profession, as set out in the ISCO classification). Some programmes take their point of departure in a particular occupation (or a limited set of occupations), and see their mission as equipping students with the knowledge and skills that are applicable to those. These are distinct from programmes that focus their mission on teaching an academic discipline, while also equipping students with a broader package of knowledge and skills based on that discipline, so that graduates are able to apply those at work, typically in a wider range of occupations.

Proposals for the development of internationally agreed definitions

This section sets out proposals for internationally agreed definitions. These proposals are based on discussions with countries and input received from countries regarding options for implementation.

Establish a three-way categorisation of programmes

The previous section described how programmes are often both "academic" and "professional", and pointed out that it would be very difficult to operationalise, for statistical purposes, the classification of programmes as more or less "academic" in the sense of intellectual complexity. It follows that the orientation of tertiary programmes needs a set of definitions focussed on professional orientation and unconnected with academic status. One point of departure is the ISCED definition of "vocational" used to identify programme orientation at ISCED levels below 5:

> **Vocational education.** *Education programmes that are designed for learners to acquire the knowledge, skills and competencies specific to a particular occupation, trade, or class of occupations or trades. Successful completion of such programmes leads to labour market-relevant vocational qualifications acknowledged as occupationally oriented by the relevant national authorities and/or the labour market. (UNESCO, 2012[19])*

The definition of "vocational" covers two types of programme, according to whether the labour market target is a "particular occupation" or a "class of occupations or trades". The same distinction is relevant at tertiary level. The proposal below is to establish categories that reflect this distinction, breaking down "professional" into two categories. One category will then include programmes that prepare for one particular profession, such as programmes training teachers, nurses or IT technicians. This needs to be distinguished from programmes that prepare for a range of jobs in a single occupational family or industry sector. This category might include, for example, a programme in environmental sciences, which might qualify an individual to work in a wide range of roles in environmental protection or environmental policy. Finally, both of the above may be distinguished from broader programmes that focus on an academic discipline such as history or mathematics, where the skills acquired may be labour market relevant, but are not specific to any one occupational or industrial sector.

The proposal here is to establish a classification based on three categories, as follows:

- Type 1: Programmes that provide applied education and training designed to equip students with knowledge and skills required to practice a particular profession.
- Type 2: Programmes that provide applied education and training designed to equip students with knowledge and skills required to work within an occupational family or industrial sector.

- Type 3: Programmes that provide discipline-oriented education in the pure sciences, humanities and arts. While such programmes will also provide knowledge and skills of labour market relevance, these are applicable in very diverse contexts and are not intended to prepare students for a particular profession, occupational family or industrial sector.

The terminology used for each category is to be agreed in consultation with countries to take into account the different nuances and resonances of particular terms in different languages. One option might be to refer to the above mentioned categories as "profession-oriented", "sector-oriented" and "general".

For simplicity, the remainder of this report will use professional to encompass both Type 1 and Type 2 (profession-oriented and sector-oriented) programmes and will refer to the three proposed categories as "profession-oriented", "sector-oriented" or "general".

Complement the classification with additional indicators to describe programmes

Using the professional specificity of programmes to define orientation provides a pragmatic approach applicable across different country and institutional contexts, and at different tertiary levels. Additional indicators would be developed to capture the diversity within the three proposed categories – measuring institutional and organisational arrangements within national education systems, as well as indicating quality. Such indicators could include, for example:

- Share of work-based learning (measured in aggregated categories, as currently collected for the categorisation of ISCED level 3 programmes).
- Share of practical content (different from work-based learning when practical content is taught in school workshops).
- Social partner engagement (e.g. involvement in the development and delivery of the programme, involvement in final assessments).

These indicators can capture important differences in programme delivery. For example, within the first category (programmes preparing for a single occupation), professional examinations include a large element of practical content and work-based learning, while some professional bachelor's or master's programmes are delivered mostly through classroom-based instruction, complemented by some work-based learning. Similarly, professional examinations in German-speaking countries are developed and delivered with substantial social partner involvement. For programmes primarily driven by provider institutions social partner engagement is certainly desirable, but is not always widespread.

- The proposed additional indicators are not definitional criteria for professional programmes, as they focus on quality-related aspects. High quality professional programmes will usually be developed and taught in close collaboration with employers, and involve work-based learning to reflect up-to-date professional practice. However, programmes designed to prepare for a profession or sector, but with limited employer engagement or no work-based learning are still professional programmes, as long as the clear intention is to prepare individuals for the profession or sector. For example, some teacher education programmes include very little classroom practice, so that novice teachers are not classroom ready. While these are serious weaknesses, it would still be appropriate to classify them as profession-oriented or sector-oriented programmes.
- The "Data collection on professional tertiary education" (see Box 1.2) included a question about the use of work-based learning within tertiary programmes (see responses in Tables 4.1 and 4.2). Based on an internationally agreed classification, further data collection could refine these answers and collect information on employer engagement (and other dimensions, if there is an interest from countries). Similarly to the typology used for vocational programmes (i.e. school-based, combined school and work-based, work-based), the information collected might underpin a more fine-grained classification of tertiary programmes. Such a classification could then be used to collect data on participation or outcomes (e.g. UOE and LSO data collections). Collecting information for all tertiary

programmes, regardless of their orientation, might also help reveal some convergence trends (e.g. growing use of internships across all programmes) or point to challenges with quality (e.g. lack of work-based learning in professional programmes).

Develop an agreed classification of detailed fields of study based on the ISCED-F framework

The ISCED-F framework could support the implementation of the proposed 3-way classification, as it contains clear and internationally agreed field of study descriptions. Agreeing on the classification of at least some fields in terms of orientation would have two benefits. First, it would allow for an unambiguous basis for the classification of some numerically large programmes leading to common occupations (e.g. teacher, nurse). As shown in Figure 1.3, these are now classified differently across countries in the absence of internationally agreed definitions, so reaching agreement would immediately improve data quality. Second, this would help with the classification of programmes in countries without clear institutional or programmatic distinctions. Numerically large fields and easy to classify fields should be a priority in the short-term.

How the classification would work in practice

Conditions underpinning classification choices

The key defining criterion for classification is the explicit objective of the programme or institution to prepare for a profession or sector. This is a necessary condition for a programme to be considered profession or sector-oriented. This may be measured by the extent to which the programme or institution is presented (e.g. website, job fairs, official documents) to students, employers and other stakeholders as preparation for a particular profession (profession-oriented) or a sector (sector-oriented). A profession may refer to an occupation within a single minor group (3-digit categories in the ISCO framework, such as engineering professionals or veterinarians) or unit group (4-digit categories in the ISCO framework, such as Nursing professionals or physiotherapists). A sector may refer to an occupational sector, such as a sub-major group (2-digit categories within the ISCO framework, e.g. science and engineering professionals) or an economic sector (ESCO category, e.g. hospitality and tourism).

Indicating such an explicit objective to prepare for a profession or sector, the following conditions are sufficient for a programme or institution to be classified as either sector or profession-oriented (the relevance of these criteria depends on the country context and the programme or institution in focus):

- **Explicit labelling of the programme or institution**: The designation of the type of programme or qualification with a professional term (e.g. professional bachelor's degree, higher vocational certificate) or of the provider institution (e.g. professional institute, college of applied arts) may indicate that a programme is profession or sector-oriented (with the name of the programme or field of study helping to identify whether it is the former or the latter). This is not a necessary condition for a programme to be considered sector or profession-oriented (in some countries multi-purpose institutions provide all sorts of tertiary programmes without specific designations for the institution or the programme type).
- **Field of study linked to a sector or profession**: The targeted field of study may indicate the target profession or sector, confirming a programme as profession or sector-oriented (or else indicate the academic discipline targeted and confirm a programme as general). This condition may be particularly helpful in countries without clear institutional or programmatic distinctions. For some fields of study there might be ambiguity, and additional indicators might be needed to help classification choices (e.g. modern languages might include training for interpreters or focus on teaching linguistics).

- **Links to regulated professions:** When licensing or registration requirements are linked to the qualification targeted by the programme, the programme is considered profession-oriented (e.g. a nursing programme leading to a qualification and license to practice as a nurse). Such linkage is a sufficient but not a necessary condition, as many professions are not subject to occupational regulation.

Application of these criteria is not mechanical, but in most cases should allow individual programmes to be classified as profession-oriented or sector-oriented. If none of the above criteria are met, the programme is general. Information available to national authorities might be variable, and will often only cover some aspects of the criteria listed above. Such national authorities may also want to classify programmes in a fairly aggregate way, recognising that within the aggregate there might be some variation in terms of orientation.

The basis for reporting might vary across countries

Across countries, professional tertiary programmes are diverse in respect of their function in the skills system, mode of delivery, and the provider institutions. Any effective classification will therefore need to be applicable in quite different institutional and programmatic contexts. To help identify the feasibility of different options, in the OECD data collection on Professional tertiary education, countries were invited to rate the suitability of different bases for reporting: i) the type of institution where programmes are provided, ii) programme as reported in ISCED mappings, or iii) detailed fields of study. While for some countries either programme or institution-based definitions are suitable, for many others only one or the other would work. In addition, several countries with unified tertiary education systems considered detailed fields of study as the most suitable tool to identify professional programmes.

The criteria set out above could be applied either at the level of provider institutions or programmes, recognising that the extent of institutional distinctions varies across countries (see Table 1.4). Countries with clear institutional distinctions may find the type of institution as the most suitable basis for distinguishing by programme orientation (e.g. universities provide general programmes, colleges sector or profession-oriented programmes). Conversely, countries that cannot rely on such institutional distinctions might find types of programmes (e.g. bachelor in applied arts, professional bachelor's degree) or targeted fields of study a more appropriate basis for reporting. The additional indicators proposed above (e.g. use of work-based learning, share of practical content) may be used to help with the classification of difficult cases. For example, programmes in languages will be profession-oriented if they include a strong element of practical training (e.g. programmes for interpreters), while pure linguistics studies will be considered general.

Testing out some examples

Some countries would be able to implement the proposed classification with relative ease, if they already define professional tertiary education in separate programmes – for example in professional bachelor's or master's degrees – or if such programmes are identifiable by the teaching institution or both (as in the case of professional bachelor's degrees obtained in Danish university colleges). There are greater challenges in the case of unified university systems as in some of the English-speaking countries. In this context, it might be necessary to use field of study information, at as granular a level as possible, to classify programmes.

At ISCED level 5 the vast majority of programmes are already reported as "professional" and the names of programmes or providers across OECD countries confirm the predominantly professional orientation of this level. Applying the more refined distinction proposed here, most could be classified as profession or sector-oriented. For example, Scottish Higher National qualifications in graphic design or photography would be profession-oriented, while those in business or health and social care would be sector-oriented. Similarly, in the Netherlands associate degrees are advertised as "professional" and could be classified as sector-oriented or profession-oriented. The few programmes that are clearly focused on an academic discipline could be classified as general (e.g. associate degree in chemistry in the United States). In addition, programmes that are often considered "higher VET" can also be identified either as profession or sector-oriented. These would include, for example, the higher vocational education system in Sweden, business academy programmes in Denmark, and the programmes delivered by Professional Colleges in Switzerland.

The growing number of professional bachelor's programmes can now be classified unambiguously. Often they are taught in UASs, and UASs may treat all of their bachelor's programmes as professional bachelor's programmes by definition. Under the definitions proposed, professional bachelor's programmes would be classified as either "profession-oriented", if they are targeted at a single profession (e.g. nurse, teacher, speech therapist, social work), or "sector-oriented", if they prepare students to work in a whole sector (e.g. international business, fashion and textile technologies, process and food technology).

Dual tertiary programmes (or tertiary apprenticeship programmes) have been growing in some countries. This includes dual study programmes in Austria and Germany, graduate apprenticeships in Scotland, degree apprenticeships in England (United Kingdom), dual study programmes in Hungary and "alternance" arrangements in France. Under these arrangements students typically spend a roughly equal amount of time in the workplace and in a higher education institution. Such dual tertiary programmes often explicitly target a specific profession (e.g. BTS pâtisserie or "Cultural guide" professional bachelor's degree in France, "Data scientist" or "Scaffold design engineer" graduate apprenticeship in Scotland), so they would normally be classified as profession-oriented. Some programmes with a broader scope would be treated as sector-oriented (e.g. professional licence "Industry professions: process improvement in automated systems" in France, "Business" graduate apprenticeship in Scotland). Finally, professional examinations (described in Box 1.5) also provide a clear case of profession-oriented programmes, as they are linked to one particular profession.

Next steps

New definitions, such as those advanced in this report, need careful development and implementation to ensure that they are workable and useful in countries, and that they are implemented consistently across countries with very different tertiary education systems. In that respect, the INES Network on labour market, economic and social outcomes of learning (LSO) may consider the final report from this project for any further steps towards developing and implementing internationally agreed definitions. These further developments, starting in 2022 after the end of this project, might involve a sequence of steps as follows:

First, the definitions set out in the report should be reviewed by both international data collection agencies, including OECD, Eurostat, ILO and UNESCO, and by individual countries to test out whether there are any prima facie issues or problems involved in the proposed definitions that need to be resolved. In the light of this initial review, any definitional changes might be considered.

Second, a test of the proposed definitions might be undertaken involving a small sample of volunteer countries with very different tertiary education systems. Support would be provided to these volunteer countries to implement the proposed definitions in their data sets on tertiary education. This would allow careful examination of how the definitions might be applied, operationally, to different types and levels of tertiary programmes. This experience would be documented by the participating countries, and difficulties or uncertainties in the implementation of the definitions identified and shared with other countries, the aim being to resolve any ambiguities in at least a consistent way across countries.

At this stage, some countries, particularly those where both profession-oriented, sector-oriented and general programmes are not separately identified as different programmes, and where they are both taught in the same institutions, might need to either develop measures to identify programme orientation from detailed field of study data, or find other ways of estimating the mix of programmes in their country.

Third, a full rollout of the definitions would be pursued with countries. The data collected would then be checked to explore any residual problems, after which the data can be used and presented in an internationally comparable way.

References

Allen, J. and B. Belfi (2020), "Educational expansion in the Netherlands: better chances for all?", *Oxford Review of Education*, Vol. 46/1, pp. 44-62, https://doi.org/10.1080/03054985.2019.1687435/SUPPL_FILE/CORE_A_1687435_SM9896.DOCX. [38]

Ayllón, S., J. Valbuena and A. Plum (2021), "Youth Unemployment and Stigmatization Over the Business Cycle in Europe", *Oxford Bulletin of Economics and Statistics*, Vol. 84/1, pp. 103-129, https://doi.org/10.1111/obes.12445. [15]

Biewen, M. and M. Thiele (2020), "Early tracking, academic vs. vocational training, and the value of 'second-chance' options", *Labour Economics*, Vol. 66, p. 101900, https://doi.org/10.1016/J.LABECO.2020.101900. [17]

Boniface, R., G. Whalley and D. Goodwin (2018), *Mapping the Higher Technical Landscape*, ation, http://www.gatsby.org.uk/uploads/education/reports/pdf/mapping-the-higher-technical-landscape-final-version.pdf (accessed on 3 June 2021). [22]

Brint, S. et al. (2005), "From the Liberal to the Practical Arts in American Colleges and Universities: Organizational Analysis and Curricular Change", *The Journal of Higher Education*, Vol. 76/2, pp. 151-180, https://doi.org/10.1353/jhe.2005.0011. [6]

Cambridge Dictionary (2020), *'Academic'*, https://dictionary.cambridge.org/dictionary/english/academic. [46]

CEDEFOP (2019), *The Changing Nature of Vocational Education and Training in Europe. Volume 6*, https://www.cedefop.europa.eu/en/publications-and-resources/publications/5570. [43]

Cedefop (2021), *Spotlight on VET - 2020 compilation: vocational education and training systems in Europe*, Publications Office of the European Union, Luxembourg, http://data.europa.eu/10.2801/10.2801/667443 (accessed on 8 February 2022). [21]

Cedefop (2014), *Employability and skills of higher education graduates*, European Commission, Brussels. [16]

Cedefop and Eurofund (2018), "Skills forecast: trends and challenges to 2030", *Cedefop reference series*, No. 108, Cedefop, https://doi.org/10.2801/4492 (accessed on 2 December 2021). [10]

Courses.ie (2021), *Courses - Find thousands of courses near you on Courses.ie*, https://www.courses.ie/ (accessed on 29 November 2021). [23]

DAAD (2021), *Universities of applied sciences*, https://www.daad.de/en/study-and-research-in-germany/plan-your-studies/hawfh/ (accessed on 5 December 2021). [34]

DIHK (2022), *Bilanzbuchhalter – Bachelor Professional in Bilanzbuchhaltung*, https://www.dihk-bildungs-gmbh.de/weiterbildung/top-weiterbildungsabschluesse/bilanzbuchhalter (accessed on 15 February 2022). [32]

European Commission (2008), *Explaining the European Qualifications Framework for Lifelong Learning*, Office for Official Publications of the European Communities, Luxembourg, https://europa.eu/europass/system/files/2020-05/EQF-Archives-EN.pdf (accessed on 8 February 2022). [20]

FAIN (2021), *Industriemeister Mechatronik IHK – Jetzt IHK-geprüften Meistertitel machen - FAIN*, https://www.fain.de/angebote/industriemeister-mechatronik-ihk (accessed on 23 November 2021). [31]

Field, S. (2018), *The missing middle: Higher technical education in England*, Gatsby Charitable Foundation, London, https://www.gatsby.org.uk/uploads/education/the-missing-middle-higher-technical-education-in-england.pdf (accessed on 12 April 2022). [44]

Gewerbeanmeldung.de (2022), "Informationen zur Gewerbeanmeldung", http://www.gewerbeanmeldung.de/meisterpflicht (accessed on 15 February 2022). [27]

Gregg, P. and E. Tominey (2005), "The wage scar from male youth unemployment", *Labour Economics*, Vol. 12/4, pp. 487-509, https://doi.org/10.1016/j.labeco.2005.05.004. [13]

Jarausch, K. (1982), "Higher Education and Social Change: Some Comparative Perspectives", in Jarausch, K. (ed.), *The transformation of higher learning 1860-1930: expansion, diversification, social opening and professionalization in England, Germany, Russia and the United States*, Klett-Cotta, Stuttgart. [2]

Kis, V. and H. Windisch (2018), "Making skills transparent: Recognising vocational skills acquired through workbased learning", *OECD Education Working Papers*, No. 180, OECD Publishing, Paris, https://doi.org/10.1787/5830c400-en. [26]

Lazerson, M. (2013), *Higher Education and the American Dream - Chapter 1. Building the dream (and worrying about it) - Central European University Press*, Central European University Press, https://books.openedition.org/ceup/795?lang=fr#notes (accessed on 26 May 2021). [3]

manQ e.K. (2022), *Master Professional - Technischer Betriebswirt (IHK)*, https://www.management-qualifizierung.de/kursangebote/betriebswirte/technischer-betriebswirt-ihk (accessed on 15 February 2022). [40]

McInnis, C. (1995), "Less Control and More Vocationalism: The Australian and New Zealand Experience", in Schuller, T. (ed.), *The Changing University?*, Taylor & Francis, Bristol, https://eric.ed.gov/?id=ED415725. [5]

MHES (2021), *About the university colleges*, https://ufm.dk/en/education/higher-education/university-colleges/about-the-university-colleges (accessed on 10 February 2022). [29]

Möller, J. and M. Umkehrer (2014), *Are there long-term earnings scars from youth unemployment in Germany?*, http://ftp.zew.de/pub/zew-docs/dp/dp14089.pdf. [14]

NCES (2021), *COE - Undergraduate Degree Fields*, https://nces.ed.gov/programs/coe/indicator/cta (accessed on 29 November 2021). [24]

OEAD (2019), *Study in Austria*, Austrian agency for international mobility and cooperation in education, science and research, http://Austrian agency for international mobility and cooperation in education, science and research (accessed on 23 December 2021). [33]

OECD (2021), *"Education at a Glance", Education and Training – Education at a Glance (database)*, https://stats.oecd.org/ (accessed on 1 June 2021). [9]

OECD (2021), *OECD Data collection on professional tertiary education*, Unpublished. [25]

OECD (2020), *OECD Employment Outlook 2020: Worker Security and the COVID-19 Crisis*, OECD Publishing, Paris, https://doi.org/10.1787/1686c758-en. [11]

OECD (2019), *OECD Employment Outlook 2019: The Future of Work*, OECD Publishing, Paris, https://doi.org/10.1787/9ee00155-en. [12]

Orientation (2021), *Les Bachelors Universitaires de Technologie (BUT) : Guide complet !*, https://www.orientation.com/diplomes/diplome-but (accessed on 23 November 2021). [30]

Oxford Languages (2020), *Google dictionary with definitions from Oxford Languages*, https://www.google.com/search?q=definition+of+%27academic%27&rlz=1C1JZAP_enFR873FR873&oq=definition+of+%27academic%27&aqs=chrome..69i57.7454j0j4&sourceid=chrome&ie=UTF-8. [45]

Prospects.ac.uk (2022), *Job profile - Patent attorney*, https://www.prospects.ac.uk/job-profiles/patent-attorney (accessed on 15 February 2022). [42]

Rait, R. (1918), *Life in the Medieval University*, Cambridge University Press, https://www.gutenberg.org/files/20958/20958-h/20958-h.htm. [1]

Schuller, T. (1995), "Introduction: The Changing University? A Sketchmap with Coda", in *The Changing University?*, Taylor & Francis, Bristol, https://files.eric.ed.gov/fulltext/ED415725.pdf (accessed on 26 May 2021). [7]

SDBB (2022), *Das offizielle schweizerische Informationsportal der Berufs-, Studien- und Laufbahnberatung*, https://www.berufsberatung.ch/ (accessed on 15 February 2022). [28]

StudieKeuze123.nl (2022), *Objectieve informatie over alle erkende hbo- en wo-opleidingen van Nederland.*, https://www.studiekeuze123.nl/ (accessed on 15 February 2022). [39]

Study in Holland (2021), *Universities of applied sciences |*, https://www.studyinholland.nl/dutch-education/universities-of-applied-sciences (accessed on 23 November 2021). [36]

studyinfo.fi (2021), *Finnish universities of applied sciences (UAS)*, https://studyinfo.fi/wp2/en/higher-education/polytechnics-universities-of-applied-sciences/ (accessed on 9 December 2021). [35]

Teichler, U. (2002), "Diversification of higher education and the profile of the individual institution", *Higher Education Management and Policy*, https://doi.org/10.1787/hemp-v14-art24-en. [4]

TU Delft (2021), *What's the difference between HBO and WO?*, https://www.tudelft.nl/en/education/information-and-experience/preparing-for-a-bachelor/whats-the-difference-between-hbo-and-wo#c244116 (accessed on 23 November 2021). [37]

Ulicna, D., K. Luomi Messerer and M. Auzinger (2016), *Study on higher Vocational Education and Training in the EU*, European Commission, Brussels, https://doi.org/10.2767/421741. [8]

UNESCO (2012), *International Standard Classification of Education ISCED 2011*, http://uis.unesco.org/sites/default/files/documents/international-standard-classification-of-education-isced-2011-en.pdf. [19]

UNESCO (2006), *ISCED 1997*, http://uis.unesco.org/sites/default/files/documents/international-standard-classification-of-education-1997-en_0.pdf. [18]

Université de Luxembourg (2022), *Formation complémentaire des candidats réviseurs d'entreprises et experts-comptables*, https://wwwfr.uni.lu/formations/fdef/formation_complementaire_des_candidats_reviseurs_d_entreprises_et_experts_comptables (accessed on 15 February 2022). [41]

Notes

[1] The data are based on the LSO data collection and country responses may not match classification choices in ISCED mappings and the UOE data collection.

[2] For analyses based on EU-LFS, Eurostat's scientific use files were used. The responsibility for all conclusions drawn from the data lies entirely with the authors.

2 Pathways into professional tertiary programmes

In a world of rising educational aspirations and increasing skill demands in the labour market, the scope for graduates of upper secondary vocational education to enter tertiary education has often become key to the attractiveness of such programmes. This chapter therefore looks first at the different access options for vocational upper secondary graduates in different countries to enter tertiary education. For some vocational upper secondary graduates, short cycle programmes provide a stepping stone to bachelor's degrees, and are often articulated to allow such progression. It also describes the employment experience of students in different types of programme, recognising that some professional tertiary programmes are designed for working adults, and often delivered part time. Data on completion rates in bachelor's level programmes are also reported.

Introduction

Professional tertiary education typically takes place at career crossroads. The entry routes include general or vocational upper secondary education, an earlier tertiary qualification or years of work experience. The exit routes, following graduation, can lead into further learning. This chapter focuses both on the routes of entry into professional programmes and the education pathways open to graduates. The analysis pays particular attention to pathways for graduates of upper secondary vocational education and training for two reasons. First, the learning opportunities open to these graduates are often more restricted than those available for general upper secondary graduates. Second, professional programmes are commonly used across OECD countries as a point of entry into tertiary education for graduates of vocational education and training (VET) in particular, while also being open to students with all kinds of educational backgrounds. The analysis looks at the programmes directly accessible for upper secondary VET graduates in different countries, as well as programmes that might be accessed upon completion of professional programmes.

The second half of the next section offers a quantitative picture of the use of these pathways. It exploits data from the European Union Labour Force Survey (EU-LFS) to show how pathways for progression are used in practice. It examines the educational background of tertiary students, the employment experience of young adults between education programmes or in parallel to tertiary studies, as well as exploring the occupations of students. The last part of this chapter looks at completion rates in tertiary programmes, recognising that dropout is a widespread challenge, in particular among students with a vocational background.

Insights from comparative data

Pathways for upper secondary VET graduates

This section focuses on access arrangements from upper secondary VET to tertiary education at ISCED level 5 and above, with particular focus on professional programmes. That is not to say that professional programmes are only for VET graduates. In many countries, professional programmes also commonly serve general upper secondary graduates, and in some countries nearly all upper secondary graduates have a general background: in Canada, New Zealand or the United States schooling is broadly comprehensive and targeted occupational training is mostly postponed until after the completion of upper secondary education. In addition, adults already holding a tertiary qualification may choose to develop technical skills in a specific area through a professional programme.

The reason for focusing specifically on access routes for upper secondary VET graduates is that for general upper secondary programmes access is not usually an issue – by definition, they are designed to prepare for higher level studies and grant eligibility to all types of tertiary programme. Vocational programmes, on the other hand, are normally primarily designed to prepare students for employment and vary, across countries and programmes, in their emphasis on preparation for further studies. Yet ensuring strong pathways from upper secondary vocational programmes to tertiary education is important for reasons related to equity, attractiveness and as a tool for raising the educational attainment of the workforce.

The equity-related reason is that education systems should ensure that nobody, at any stage in their lives, should be locked out of higher level learning opportunities. It would be wrong to say that VET graduates 'should' pursue tertiary studies. High-quality VET programmes should equip young people with skills for an entry level job and prepare them for successful careers. However, while not all VET graduates will pursue tertiary studies, that option should be present. VET graduates must also be equipped with the right skills, so that they can not only enter tertiary programmes, but also succeed in them, and use these further learning opportunities to realise rewarding careers. Having opportunities for higher level learning could make VET a more attractive pathway to students at the upper-secondary level, keeping the options for students open and avoiding VET programmes to be or be seen as dead-ends.

Increasing the tertiary attainment rate among working age adults is a common objective for countries seeking to improve workforce skills. The European Union's new target for 2030 is that the share of 30-34 year-olds with a tertiarz qualification should reach 45%. In countries that make extensive use of vocational programmes at upper secondary level (see Figure 2.1), raising tertiary attainment requires engaging a higher share of VET graduates in tertiary education. Professional programmes can offer an attractive form of tertiary education to VET graduates, allowing them to obtain advanced technical and managerial skills. According to estimates based on the OECD Survey of Adult Skills, a product of the Programme for the International Assessment of Adult Competencies (PIAAC), upper secondary VET graduates are more likely to pursue occupations that face a high risk of automation than tertiary graduates (Vandeweyer and Verhagen, 2020[1]). Many other jobs are likely to be drastically reshaped as a result of automation. To adapt to this changing work environment, any VET graduates will therefore need to upskill or reskill in the course of their careers, and professional programmes, particularly if they are delivered part-time or flexibly, will allow them to achieve this objective.

Figure 2.1. Share of upper secondary students graduating from a vocational programme (2018)

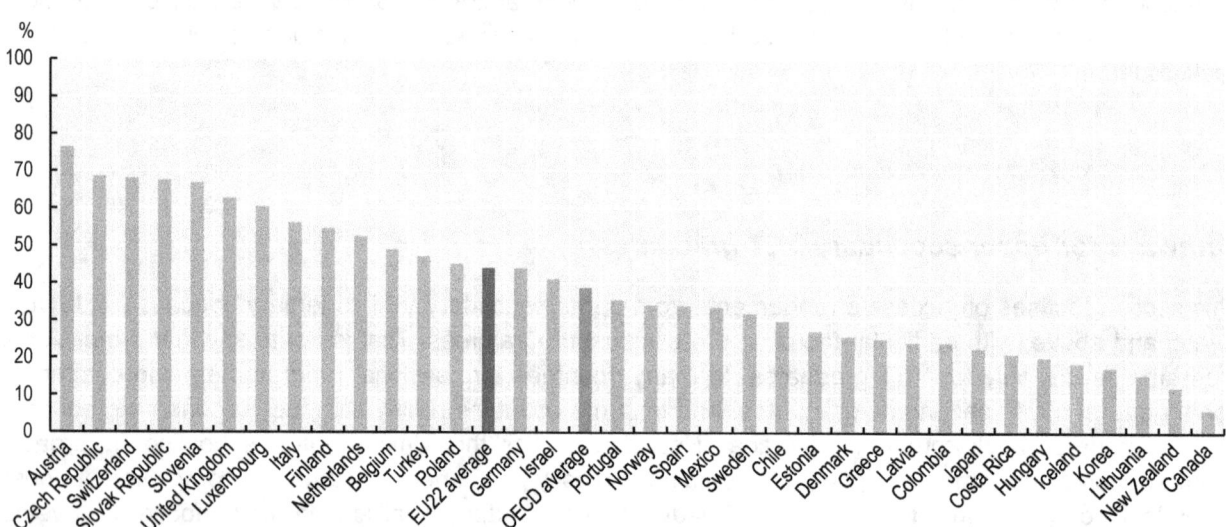

Source: OECD (2020[2]), "Education at a Glance", Education and Training – Education at a Glance (database), https://stats.oecd.org/.

StatLink https://stat.link/zr8pvc

Figure 2.2. Distribution of students enrolled in upper secondary VET by access to tertiary education

Full- and part-time students enrolled in public and private institutions

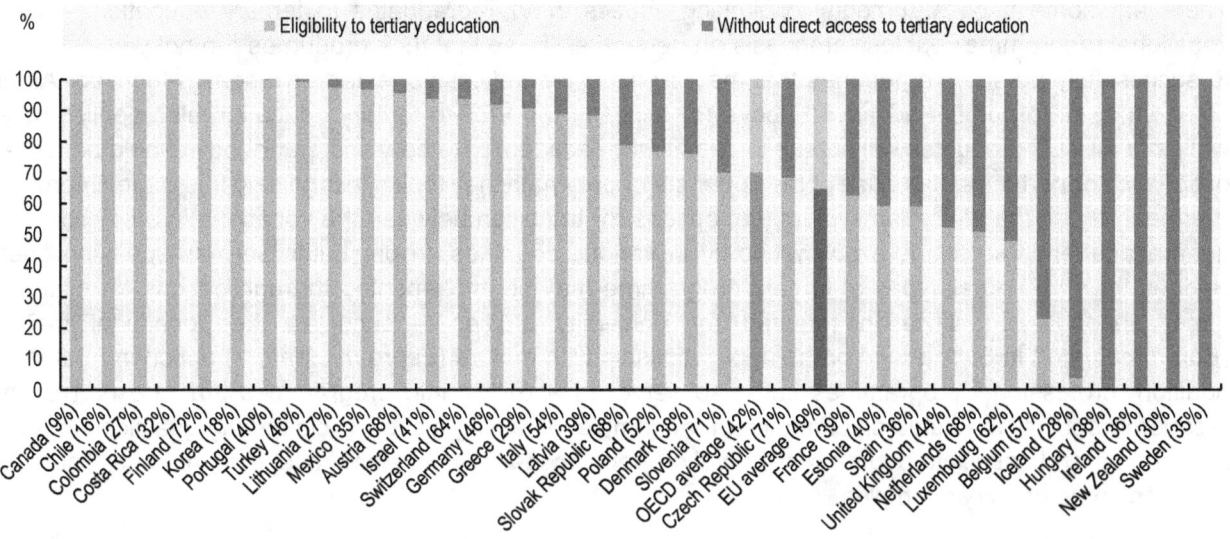

Note: Figures in parentheses refer to the share of students enrolled in upper secondary vocational education as a percentage of all students enrolled at this level.
Source: OECD (2020[3]), *Education at a Glance 2020: OECD Indicators*, https://doi.org/10.1787/69096873-en.

StatLink https://stat.link/hovdc2

On average across OECD countries, 70% of upper-secondary VET students are enrolled in programmes that give direct access to tertiary education (Figure 2.2 Figure 2.1). Typically, in countries and programmes where vocational upper secondary qualifications do not provide direct access to tertiary education, there are options to gain eligibility (e.g. bridging courses, recognition of prior learning). The term "direct access to tertiary education" means that graduates have access to some or all programmes at a one or more higher ISCED levels. Behind this term, many countries have a more nuanced set of access arrangements. In many countries (e.g. Czech Republic, Estonia, France, Latvia, Lithuania, Norway, Slovak Republic, Slovenia, Sweden) the qualification(s) required for tertiary studies yield access to all types of tertiary education. In some, however, graduates of some (or all) vocational programmes have access to some types of tertiary education only, typically professional programmes, programmes in universities of applied sciences and/or shorter tertiary programmes. Table 2.1 provides some examples. In the absence of internationally agreed definitions, and the resulting cross-country variation in classification choices, it is not possible to distinguish access options as "access to professional programmes only" as opposed to "access to both academic and professional programmes" – for example UAS programmes are classified as academic in Switzerland and as having "unspecified orientation" in the Netherlands, although presumably similar. However, in some countries VET programmes yield access only to a particular set of programmes, which are often provided in a separate tier of tertiary education institutions such as universities of applied science or university colleges, not regular universities.

In some cases, upper secondary VET graduates may only access short-cycle tertiary programmes, although those programmes may then serve as a bridge into bachelor's programmes. For example, in Austria graduates of school-based upper secondary VET (year 1-3 of BHS programmes) have direct access to year 4-5 of BHS, which is considered short-cycle tertiary education. Similarly, in Flanders, vocational upper secondary education provides direct access to associate degree, but not ISCED 6 programmes. In other cases direct access from upper secondary VET is only possible to certain programmes at ISCED level 6. For example, in the Netherlands VET graduates have direct access to bachelor's (or associate degree) programmes provided by UAS-s, but not to bachelor's programmes at regular universities.

There are some good arguments for limiting access of VET graduates to tertiary education – some vocational programmes put less emphasis on general skills, so that their graduates are not well-prepared to successfully pursue programmes that may be more theoretically-oriented or research-focused. At the same time, the argument advanced above for access from VET to tertiary education also applies here: while not all VET graduates will pursue studies in the "academic" tertiary sector, nobody should be locked out of such opportunities because of the upper secondary path they took. Recognising this issue, improving "permeability" in the education system (i.e. options for transition between the vocational/professional and general/academic sector) is a policy priority in various countries, in particular German-speaking ones. Bridges from VET to all types of tertiary programme may be implemented through options to obtain an upper secondary qualification required for university studies – such as the vocational matura (*Berufsmaturität*) in Switzerland or the apprenticeship with matura (*Lehre mit Matura*) option in Austria. In addition, professional programmes can also serve as a bridge into programmes that are part of the "academic sector". In Austria and Flanders, for example, obtaining a short-cycle tertiary qualification (BHS programme and associate degree respectively) opens access to bachelor's level programmes. Table 2.1 provides some country examples.

Table 2.1. Professional programmes as a path from VET into academic programmes

Country	Upper secondary vocational programme	Tertiary programme(s) directly accessible	Progression options into "academic" tertiary programmes via professional programmes
Austria	BHS years 1-3	BHS years 4-5 (ISCED 5)	Graduates of years 4-5 may pursue further studies at a university or a university of applied science.
Belgium (Flanders)	Vocational upper secondary (BSO-6 years)	Associate degree (ISCED 5)	Associate degree graduates have direct access to both professional and academic bachelor's programmes.
Denmark	Vocational upper secondary	Academy profession (ISCED 5) and some professional bachelor's programmes.	Academy profession graduates may pursue programmes at a higher ISCED level within the same field. For graduates at level 6 this also includes academic programmes at ISCED 7 (see also ISCED mapping).
Germany	Dual system	Professional tertiary programmes (e.g. Master craftsman programmes, trade and technical schools, Kindergarten teacher training)	Graduates of professional tertiary programmes have direct access to academic bachelor's programmes at universities or universities of applied science, even if they do not hold the usually required upper secondary qualification (*Abitur*).
Netherlands	Vocational upper secondary	Universities of applied sciences	Upon completion of the first year of a UAS programme, students may transition into the first year of a regular university.
Switzerland	Dual system 3-4 year programmes	PET college, professional examinations	Individuals holding a professional qualification may be able to access programmes in universities of applied sciences, but admission not automatic. Recommendations have been made for the admission of applicants with a professional qualification to a bachelor's programme, but the admission decision is taken by individual institutions.

Source: OECD Data collection on professional tertiary education.

Graduates of short-cycle tertiary programmes who wish to progress to higher level studies should be able to have learning outcomes from these short-cycle programmes recognised through access and course exemptions. Articulation between short-cycle and bachelor's level programmes varies across countries.

For example, in France there are clear pathways between the two levels (see Box 2.1). In several countries some, but not all programmes, have articulation arrangements with bachelor's level programmes: in Denmark, graduates of some (but not all) academy profession programmes have the option of pursuing a top-up programme of 1.5 years to obtain a professional bachelor's degree, in Scotland (United Kingdom) some HNC-s and some HND-s allow direct entry into the first or second year of degree programmes, and in Belgium (Flemish Community) the recently created associate degree programmes also allow articulation into bachelor's programmes depending on their education background and the university college.

But such articulation arrangements often depend on individual institutions, and are not systematic. A study of higher VET in Europe noted the insufficient recognition of learning outcomes from short-cycle programmes (as well as postsecondary non-tertiary programmes) in bachelor's level tertiary education (Ulicna, Luomi Messerer and Auzinger, 2016[4]). Sometimes short-cycle tertiary programmes and higher levels of education belong to different sectors in terms of governance, making transitions difficult. Provider institutions have to laboriously negotiate articulation arrangements on a programme by programme, and institution by institution basis, and may have few incentives to grant course exemptions. Students have to repeat course material, if they are not deterred from further studies by the prospect of repetition. A multinational review of professional programmes across OECD countries argued that building articulation frameworks, supported by transparency and quality measures is important to reduce such inefficiencies in national skills systems (OECD, 2014[5]).

> **Box 2.1. Articulation between ISCED level 5 and 6 programmes in France**
>
> Professional bachelor's programmes usually take three years to complete. Students who have completed one year of studies at ISCED level 5 in a relevant field and validated 60 ECTS, obtain a professional bachelor's qualification after two years of additional studies. Those who completed a two-year programme, which yields 120 ECTS, need to pursue only one additional year of study to obtain a professional bachelor's degree.
>
> Given the widespread use of the progression path from two year technological diplomas (DUT) to professional bachelor's degrees (over 85% of DUT graduates moved on to complete a professional bachelor's programme), the two programmes were consolidated in 2020 through the introduction of three-year "bachelor of technology" (BUT) qualifications.
>
> Source: Onisep (2022[6]), *Les licences professionnelles*, https://www.onisep.fr/Choisir-mes-etudes/Apres-le-bac/Organisation-des-etudes-superieures/Les-licences-professionnelles; OECD (2021[7]), *OECD Data collection on professional tertiary education*, Unpublished.

Progression patterns between different levels of education and training

Ideally, comparative data would be available to track the progression of upper secondary graduates through postsecondary or tertiary education and the labour market. But comparative cross-sectional data typically only record the highest qualification attained by individuals and therefore contain little information about the pathway to that qualification. At the country level, some OECD countries have longitudinal surveys and/or tracer surveys that allow more in-depth analysis of pathways. This section explores progression patterns using data from the UOE data collection as well as the European Union Labour Force Survey (EU-LFS), to paint a picture of how students with different profiles enter and progress within tertiary education. One limitation of these data is that they distinguish only between levels of education and training, not the orientation of programmes. This allows for the identification of short-cycle tertiary programmes, which are treated as professional in this report, but professional programmes cannot be identified for ISCED level 6 and above. Figure 2.3 shows the level at which individuals start their first tertiary programme. Short-cycle tertiary programmes are a major point of entry into tertiary education in some countries (e.g. Austria, Chile, Turkey, Spain). While not represented in this figure, in the United States around 40% of new entrants start their education in a community college (Shapiro et al., 2017[8]), through an associate degree. By contrast, in many OECD countries short-cycle tertiary programmes play a small role. Overall, the majority of students across OECD countries start tertiary studies at bachelor's level. A very small share of students start their tertiary studies via "long first-degree programmes" (e.g. in Europe following the implementation of the Bologna process such programmes have become less common, they often include 5-6 year programmes in specific fields like medicine). As these data refer to new entrants only, they do not capture individuals who already studied at the tertiary level and re-entered for upskilling, reskilling or other purposes.

Figure 2.3. Distribution of new entrants by tertiary level (2018)

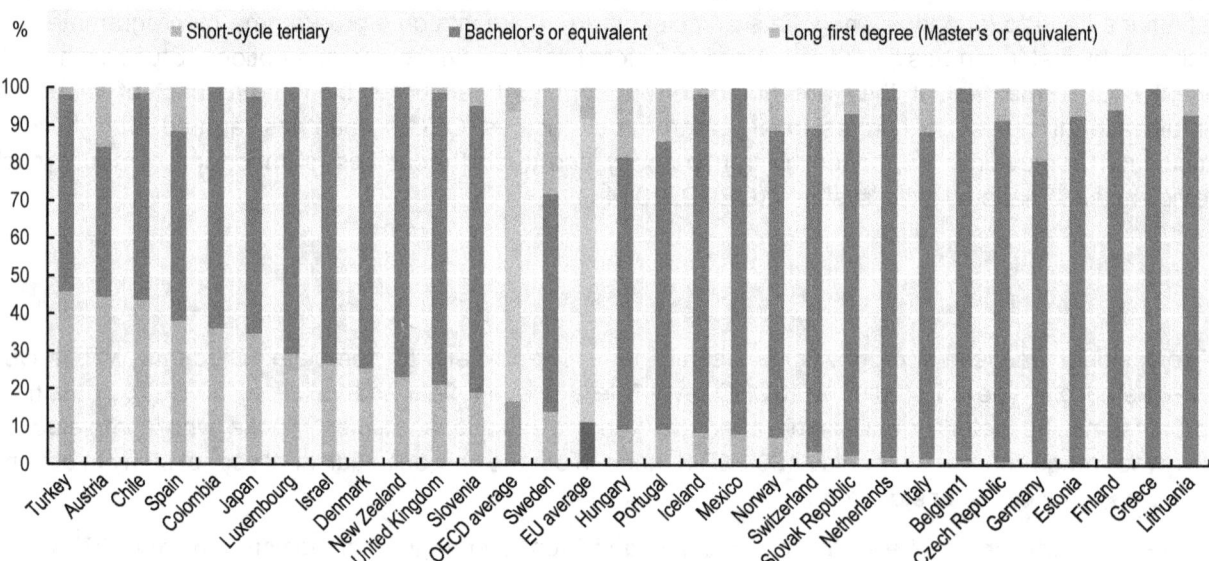

1. Data for Belgium for short-cycle tertiary refer to the Flemish Community only.
Source: OECD (2020[3]), *Education at a Glance 2020: OECD Indicators*, https://doi.org/10.1787/69096873-en.

StatLink ⏵ https://stat.link/9hdcjn

To shed some light on the educational background of tertiary students, Figure 2.4 shows the highest prior qualification of current students in short-cycle tertiary programmes (for EU countries only). In some countries (e.g. Austria, Slovenia, Italy, Croatia), short-cycle tertiary programmes mainly serve graduates of the upper secondary VET system. But in most countries VET graduates account for a minority of students at this level, and programmes enrol students with a general upper secondary background (and even a prior tertiary qualification). As these data are based on the highest qualification of individuals, the general upper secondary or postsecondary or tertiary category will sometimes include VET graduates who entered short-cycle programmes via these other programmes. For example, when VET graduates pursue a bridging course to gain eligibility for tertiary education, and therefore report that course as their highest qualification, they will appear under the "general upper secondary or postsecondary" category. In Norway, for example, such preparatory courses (which may be taken after a four-year vocational programme) yield a general upper secondary qualification, and therefore more short-cycle tertiary students may hold a VET qualification than the figure suggests.

Figure 2.4. Distribution of educational attainment of students in short-cycle tertiary programmes (2017-2019 pooled)

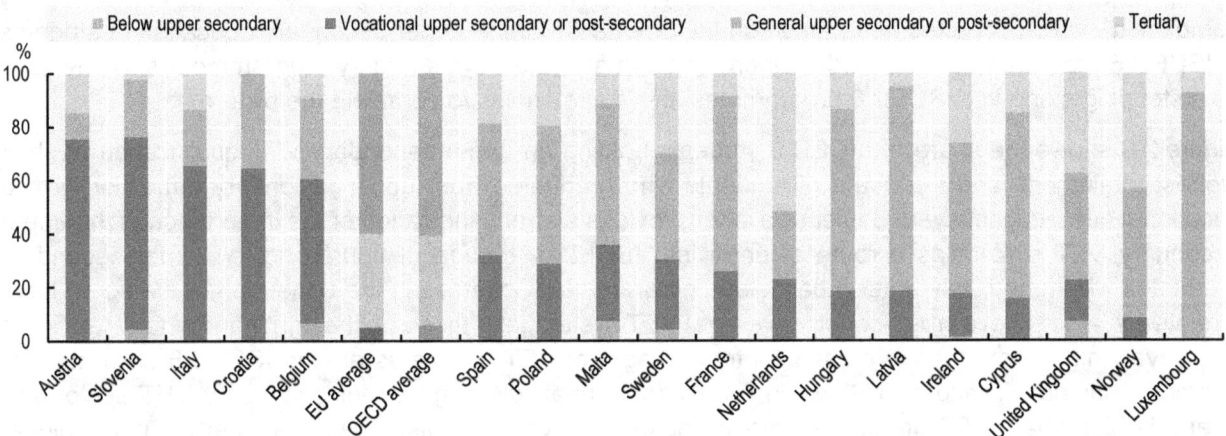

Note: Data include only students aged 34 or less or who obtained their highest qualification up to 15 years prior to the survey. Averages refer to unweighted averages of available countries.
Source: European Union Labour Force Survey (2017, 2018, 2019).

StatLink https://stat.link/hxy4v8

Figure 2.5 shows the prior attainment of current bachelor's level students. In most cases, bachelor's level students come directly from upper secondary education (the extent to which they pursue employment in between is discussed below). Pursuing short-cycle tertiary education before entering ISCED 6 programmes is common in only a few countries (e.g. Austria, Sweden, Spain, France, United Kingdom). In some of those countries short-cycle tertiary programmes appear to be used by VET graduates for transition into bachelor's level programmes. For example, in Austria, France, Malta, Spain and Sweden short-cycle tertiary graduates comprise over 10% of ISCED 6 students, while upper secondary VET graduates account for over a quarter of short-cycle tertiary students (see Figure 2.4).

Figure 2.5. Distribution of educational attainment of students in ISCED level 6 programmes (2017- 2019 pooled)

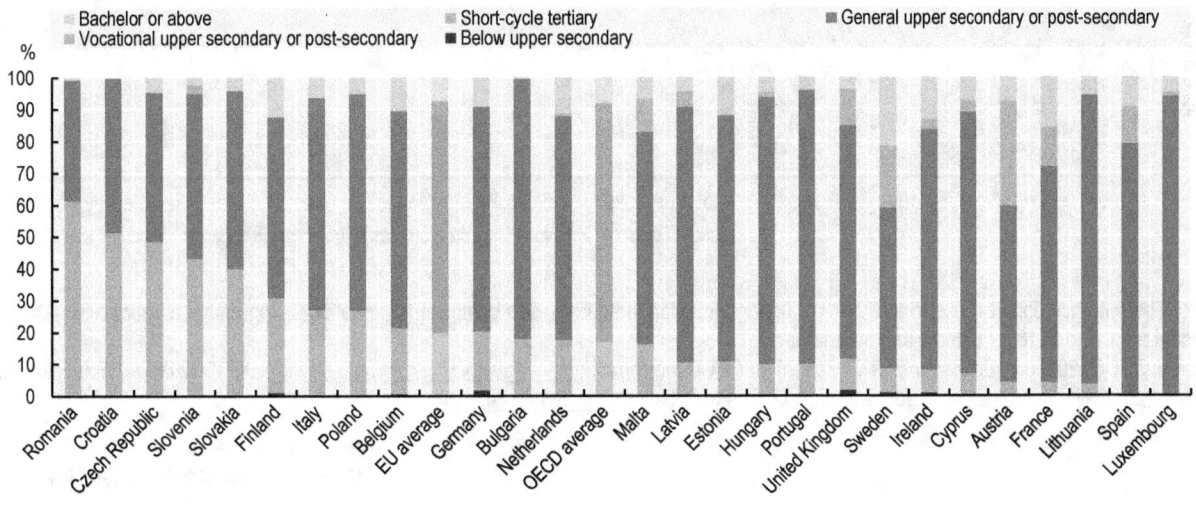

Note: Data include only students aged 34 or less or who obtained their highest qualification up to 15 years prior to the survey. Averages refer to unweighted averages of available countries.
Source: European Union Labour Force Survey (2017, 2018, 2019).

StatLink https://stat.link/pw1ou8

As explained above, the available comparative data, based on highest qualification, provide poor measures of the use of short-cycle tertiary programmes as a pathway from upper secondary education into bachelor's level programmes. However, some insights can be gained from the "OECD Ad hoc survey on tertiary completion", which collected information on the orientation of the upper secondary education of students in ISCED 6 programmes. In countries where bridging and short-cycle tertiary programme are widely used as a stepping stone into ISCED 6 programmes, this survey helps to complete the picture.

Figure 2.6 shows the share of ISCED 6 students holding an upper secondary VET qualification as their highest attainment, and the share of students who graduated from upper secondary education with a vocational qualification a year earlier (the latter provides a strong indication of the importance of the upper secondary VET system as a route of entry into ISCED 6, though of course not all upper secondary graduates will immediately enter a bachelor's programme). Countries in the upper half of the figure have a relatively large (above cross-country average) VET system, and those on the right hand side of the figure a relatively high share (above cross-country average) of VET graduates among ISCED 6 students. For example, Austria, Finland and Slovenia have both a relatively large upper secondary VET sector and relatively high share VET graduates among bachelor's level students. In Austria clearly a much higher share of ISCED 6 students have a vocational background than suggested by the attainment data in Figure 2.5 – indeed national data show over one in four university students and over 50% of UAS (*Fachhochschule*) students have a vocational qualification (mostly BHS) (Statistik Austria, 2021[9]).

Figure 2.6. Relationship between the share of graduates from upper secondary vocational programmes and their share in the entrance cohort at bachelor's level (2017)

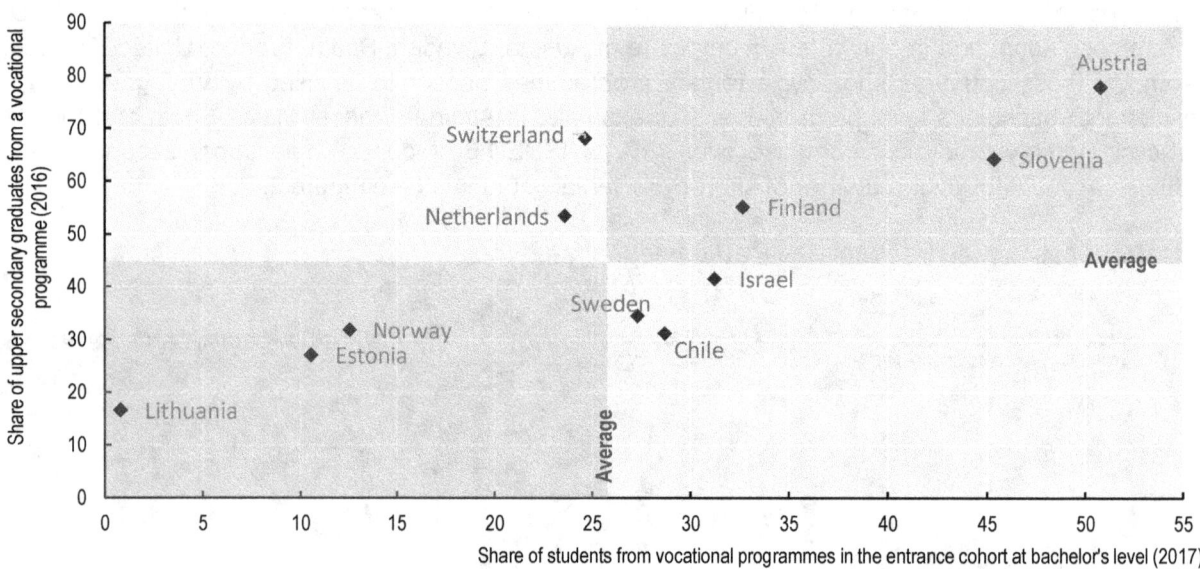

Note: The entrance cohort refers to the share of upper secondary graduates who completed a vocational programme a year earlier. Data on graduates refer to 2018 for Estonia and Switzerland.
Source: OECD (2019[10]), *Education at a Glance 2019: OECD Indicators*, https://doi.org/10.1787/f8d7880d-en; OECD (2020[2]), "Education at a Glance", Education and Training – Education at a Glance (database), https://stats.oecd.org/.

StatLink https://stat.link/0yi4h2

Several countries have implemented measures designed to assist VET and sometimes professional tertiary graduates to progress into higher levels of education. These include various tools, such as adjusting admission criteria to take into account relevant work experience, lowering academic entry requirements or using quotas (see Box 2.2 for some examples).

> ### Box 2.2. Making professional programmes more accessible to VET graduates
>
> **Portugal**
>
> For the 2020/21 academic year, 2 615 new places were reserved for students who completed upper secondary education via vocational pathways and specialised arts courses. This new access route is designed to broaden the social base of higher education, where VET graduates are currently underrepresented. The target for 2023 is that 40% of those who graduate from VET enter higher education. In addition, there is a target for adult participation: they should account for 10% of new students at polytechnics and universities by 2023.
>
> **Denmark**
>
> Admission to higher education is based on a system of "Coordinated Admission", which involves two quotas designed to make professional programmes more accessible for applicants with lower GPA-s. One set of places (quota 1) are allocated based solely on GPA performance in the upper secondary examination. An additional set of places (quota 2) are allocated based on the assessment of individual institutions: they take into account additional criteria, such as work experience, volunteer work, other qualifications, admission tests or interviews. While the allocation of quotas varies between study programmes, professional programmes represent a higher share of quota 2 places than academic programmes.
>
> **Lithuania**
>
> While applicants to all tertiary programmes are required to have a secondary education diploma and pass secondary school examinations, admission requirements to colleges are less demanding than to universities (i.e. lower grades and fewer examinations). In addition, a vocational qualification yields extra points in the admission system for colleges.
>
> Source: OECD Data collection on professional tertiary education.

Employment experience among students

Progression between different levels of education sometimes involves spells of employment between programmes, or parallel to studies. Across different countries and programmes, the extent of work experience and its nature (relevant to a vocational qualification or not) varies greatly. Work experience may build on an earlier (typically vocational) qualification and, as a person's career progresses, lead into an advanced programme to deepen or broaden skills linked to their occupation. This is common among adults pursuing master craftsman qualifications and other professional examinations, which are open only to experienced professionals who typically continue working while preparing for their examination. In other cases, individuals have work experience that does not build on vocational skills, either because the person does not have a vocational qualification or pursued employment unrelated to their qualification. Such work experience can still develop useful generic skills, like team work or conflict management, but it does not play a role of building up technical skills, on which a higher level, professional qualification might build. Some of that experience will be student jobs, pursued to financially support ongoing studies, and periods of employment before engaging in further studies.

This section exploits data from the European Union Labour Force Survey to look at the work experience of students. The data cover both the current work and past employment experience of students. Including current employment is important, as in professional programmes in some countries it is very common to work parallel to pursuing tertiary studies (see Chapter 3 on part-time participation). In the analysis past and current employment are grouped to allow for sufficiently large sample sizes. Ideally, data would also show whether current studies are in the same field as the prior qualification, revealing whether studies are used for progression within the same sector or for a career shift. Unfortunately, this is not possible with the EU-LFS dataset, as data on the current fields of study are no longer collected.

> **Box 2.3. Analysing the employment experience of students with EU-LFS data**
>
> For students who are in work, the analysis uses their current occupation. For students who are not in work, the dataset allows to identify whether they have previous employment experience. Such previous experience excludes compulsory military or civil service and purely occasional work. The latest occupation is the occupation in their previous job.
>
> The occupations held by students are grouped into four categories:
>
> - High-skilled white collar: managers, professionals, technicians and associate professionals.
> - High-skilled blue collar: Skilled agricultural, forestry and fishery workers, craft and related trades workers.
> - Low-to-medium skilled white collar: Clerical support workers, service and sales workers.
> - Low-to-medium skilled blue collar: Plant and machine operators, and assemblers, elementary occupations.

Among short-cycle tertiary students it is relatively common to have employment experience, especially among students with a vocational upper secondary background (see Figure 2.7). On average over 60% of short-cycle tertiary students with a VET background either work parallel to their studies or have worked in the past.

For VET graduates the question arises to what extent they work in skilled occupations, which may build on their vocational qualification. Figure 2.8 shows the latest occupation held by current short-cycle tertiary students with a vocational upper secondary qualification. Data for general upper secondary graduates are not included here, because sample sizes were too small for most countries and the question of the relevance of the earlier occupational qualification does not arise for general education graduates. It shows that at least a quarter of VET graduates in short-cycle tertiary programmes hold (or held in their last job) a high-skilled white collar in the Netherlands, the United Kingdom, France, Sweden and Austria. In addition, a considerable share (between 15 and 25%) of VET graduates have held high-skilled blue-collar occupations in France, Austria, Slovenia and Spain. Finally, some of the occupations in the low-to-medium skilled category might be related to vocational qualifications, as some programmes in the field of business and management prepare for jobs as "service and sales" and "clerical support" workers.

Figure 2.7. Share of short-cycle tertiary students with employment experience (2017-2019 pooled)

Current students with ISCED 3-4 attainment who are employed or have previous employment experience, by orientation of prior qualification

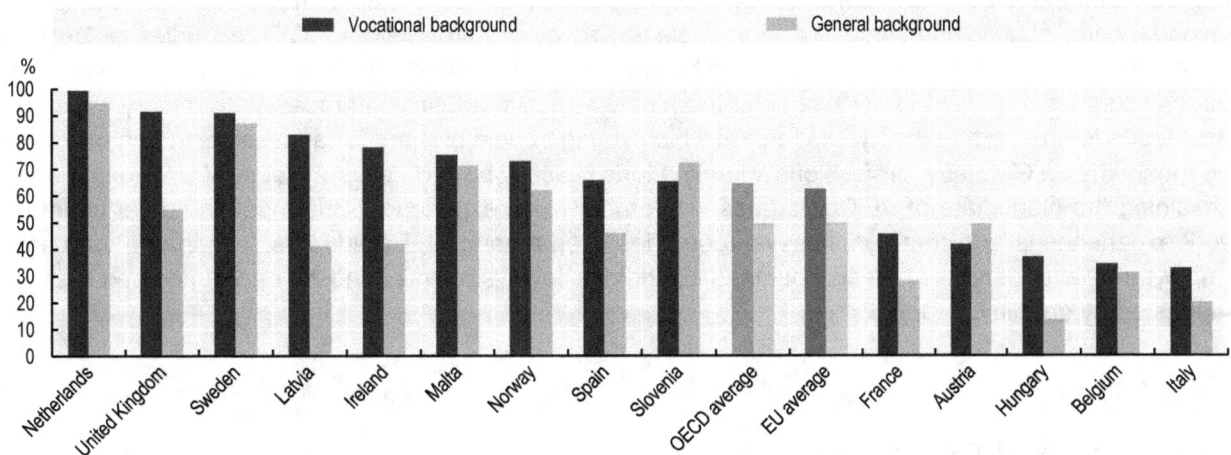

Note: Data include only individuals whose highest qualification is ISCED 3 or 4, and are aged less than 35 or obtained their highest qualification up to 15 years before the survey. Averages refer to unweighted averages of available countries. Purely occasional work, such as vacation work, compulsory military or community service are excluded.
Source: European Union Labour Force Survey (2017, 2018, 2019).

StatLink https://stat.link/m2r5ow

Figure 2.8. Latest occupation held by ISCED 5 students with a VET background (2017-2019 pooled)

Current or last occupation held by students with vocational upper secondary or postsecondary attainment

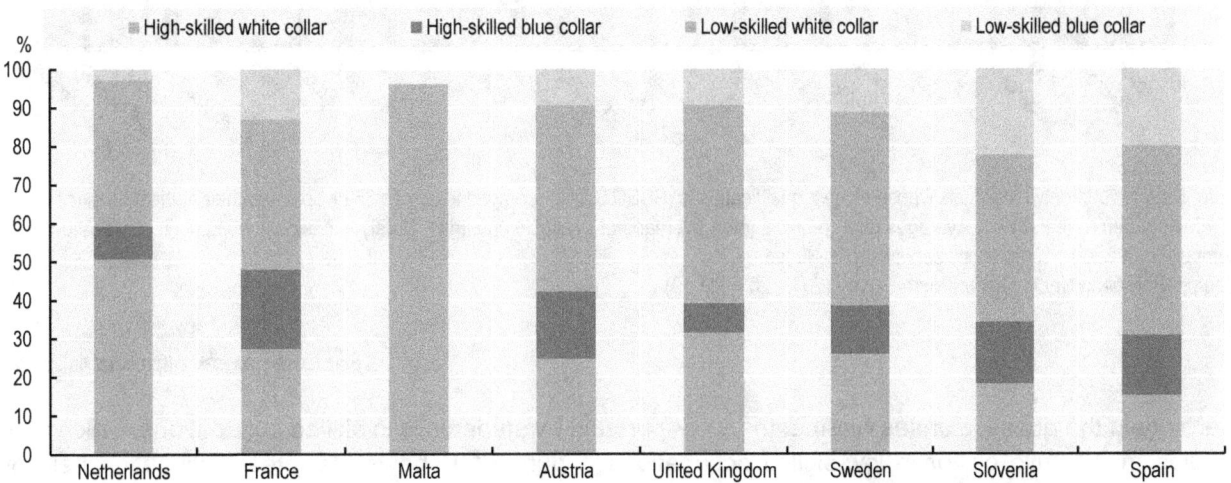

Note: Data include only individuals aged 34 or less or who obtained their highest qualification up to 15 years before the survey. Averages refer to unweighted averages of available countries. Data for Malta have limited reliability due to small sample sizes. Data are presented only for countries with at least two categories above the publication threshold for reliability. Categories may not add up to 100% because data below the publication threshold for reliability are excluded.
Source: European Union Labour Force Survey (2017, 2018, 2019).

StatLink https://stat.link/w8p37c

Among countries with data available both for ISCED 5 and ISCED 6 students, the share of students with past or current work experience is similar on average for both categories. For the larger set of countries covered by Figure 2.10, the share of students having work experience is lower on average. As illustrated by Figure 2.9, students with a prior vocational qualification more commonly have employment experience than students with a general upper secondary background (this chart excludes those who gained an upper secondary qualification and pursued a short-cycle tertiary programme before ISCED 6 studies, as only the highest qualification of individuals is captured by the data). The results reflect different underlying reasons across countries – in Finland, for example, the highly selective admission process into tertiary education often leads to one or more gap years, during which young people prepare for admission and often work in the meantime. In Germany, professional examinations typically build on several years of work experience, explaining the high share of VET graduates with employment experience. But in several other countries work experience is less common, in seven countries even among VET graduates, less than a third have employment experience (in these countries bachelor's level students tend to be younger as well, as suggested by data in Chapter 3).

Figure 2.9. Share of ISCED level 6 students with employment experience (2017-2019 pooled)

Current students with ISCED 3-4 attainment who are employed or have previous employment experience, by orientation of prior attainment

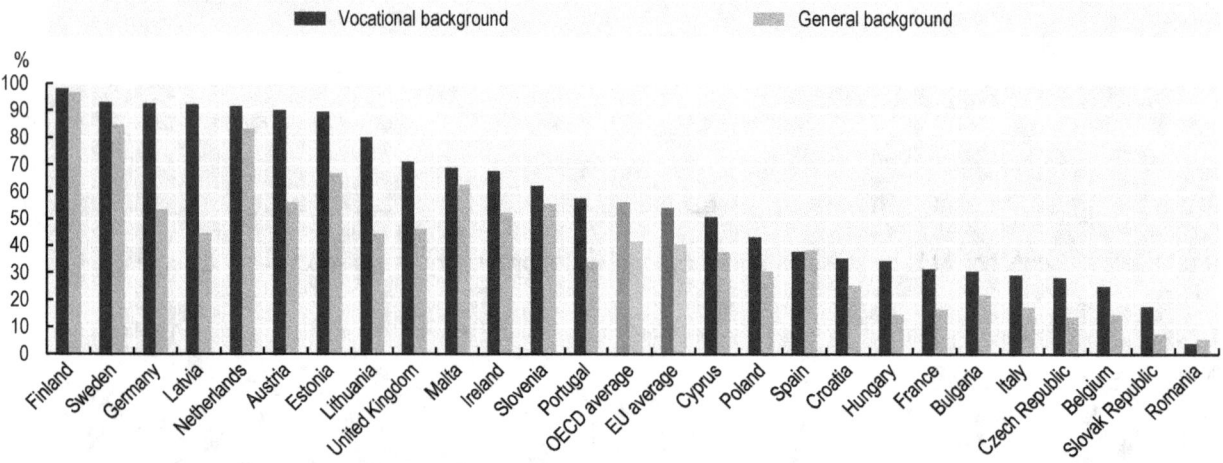

Note: Data include only individuals whose highest qualification is ISCED 3 or 4, are aged less than 35 or obtained their highest qualification up to 15 years before the survey. Averages refer to unweighted averages of available countries. Purely occasional work, such as vacation work, compulsory military or community service are excluded.
Source: European Union Labour Force Survey (2017, 2018, 2019).

StatLink https://stat.link/6tornc

Here again the question arises whether the work pursued by students is in skilled occupations, which their studies might build on, or in low-skilled occupations. Figure 2.10 shows the latest occupation held by students pursuing an ISCED 6 qualification for students with a vocational vs. general upper secondary background. In Latvia, Austria and Germany around 90% of VET graduates who pursue an ISCED 6 programme have current or past work experience and mostly in high-skilled occupations. Within high-skilled occupations, having employment experience in white-collar occupations is more common among ISCED 6 students than in blue-collar occupations. On average, over 40% of VET graduates who pursue ISCED 6 programmes hold (or held as their last occupation) a high-skilled job. This share is higher than for general upper secondary graduates, among whom about 30% work or worked in a high-skilled occupation (see Figure 2.11).

Figure 2.10. Latest occupation held by ISCED level 6 students with a vocational background (2017-19 pooled)

Current or last occupation held by students with vocational upper secondary or postsecondary attainment

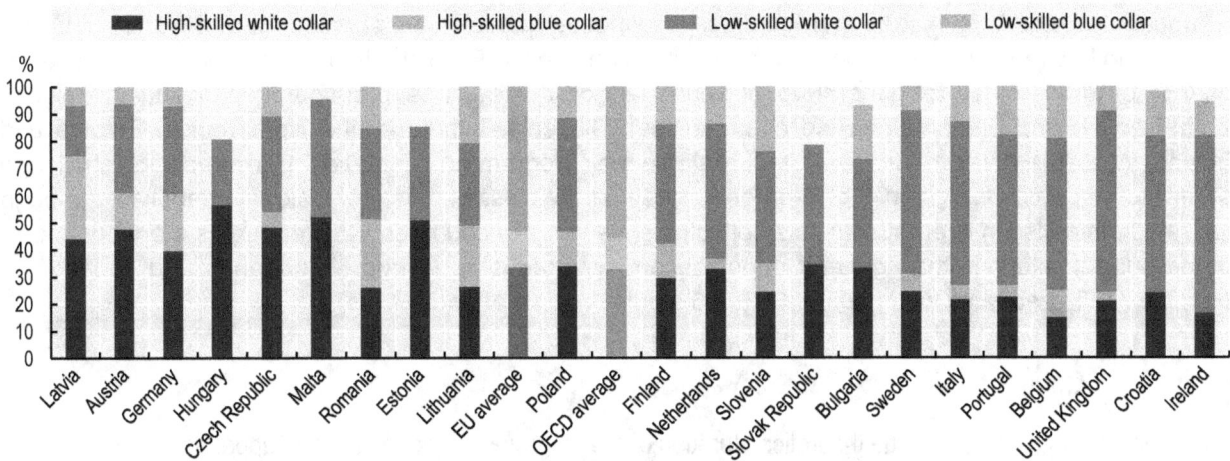

Note: Data include only individuals who are aged 34 or less or obtained their highest qualification up to 15 years before the survey. Averages refer to unweighted averages of available countries. Data are presented only for countries with at least two categories above the publication threshold for reliability. Categories may not add up to 100% because data below the publication threshold for reliability are excluded.
Source: European Union Labour Force Survey (2017, 2018, 2019).

StatLink https://stat.link/56wf9h

Figure 2.11. Latest occupation held by ISCED level 6 students with a general education background (2017-2019 pooled)

Current or last occupation held by students with general upper secondary or postsecondary attainment

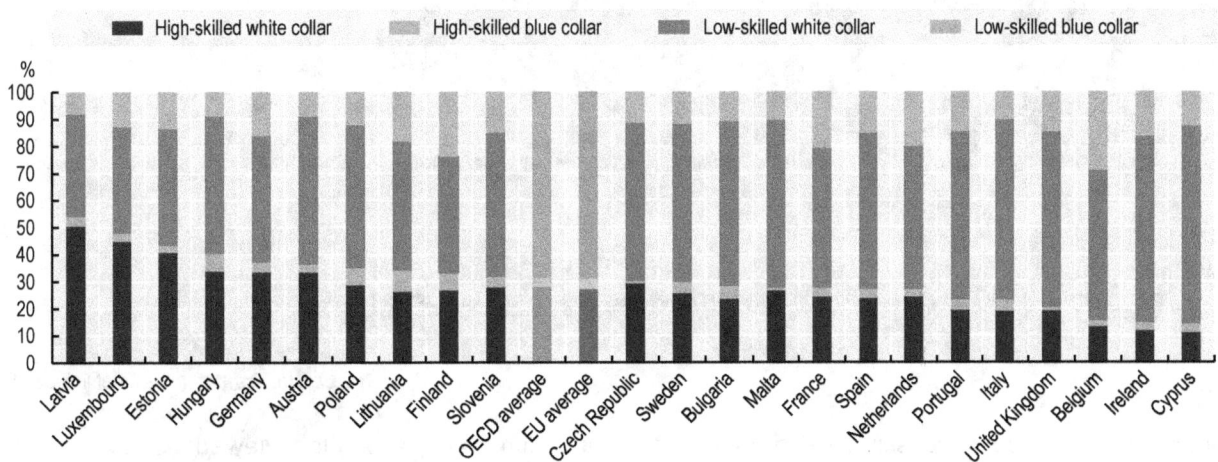

Note: Data include only individuals who are aged 34 or less or obtained their highest qualification up to 15 years before the survey. Averages refer to unweighted averages of available countries.
Source: European Union Labour Force Survey (2017, 2018, 2019).

StatLink https://stat.link/09dsul

Completion rates in bachelor's level programmes

Achieving high completion rates in tertiary education is a widespread challenge, especially for students with a vocational background (see Figure 2.12). Data from the OECD "Ad hoc survey on tertiary completion" provide completion rates for students in bachelor's level programmes and allow for distinction by upper secondary background (regardless of whether participants pursued at ISCED level 4 or 5 programme between their upper secondary qualification and ISCED 6 studies). Completion rates are lower for VET graduates than for general upper secondary graduates in several countries, including Belgium (both Flemish and French Speaking communities), Slovenia, Lithuania, the Netherlands, Estonia and Finland. While the data do not allow for a breakdown by programme orientation, the completion challenge is likely to be particularly prominent in programmes that are classified as professional or applied, although classified otherwise in international data collections, as in many countries VET graduates more commonly attend such institutions than general upper secondary graduates (in the Netherlands and Finland, for example, VET graduates who pursue ISCED 6 studies mainly attend UAS-s).

Figure 2.12. Completion rate of ISCED level 6 students (2017)

Completion within 3 years after the theoretical duration of the programme by orientation of upper secondary qualification.

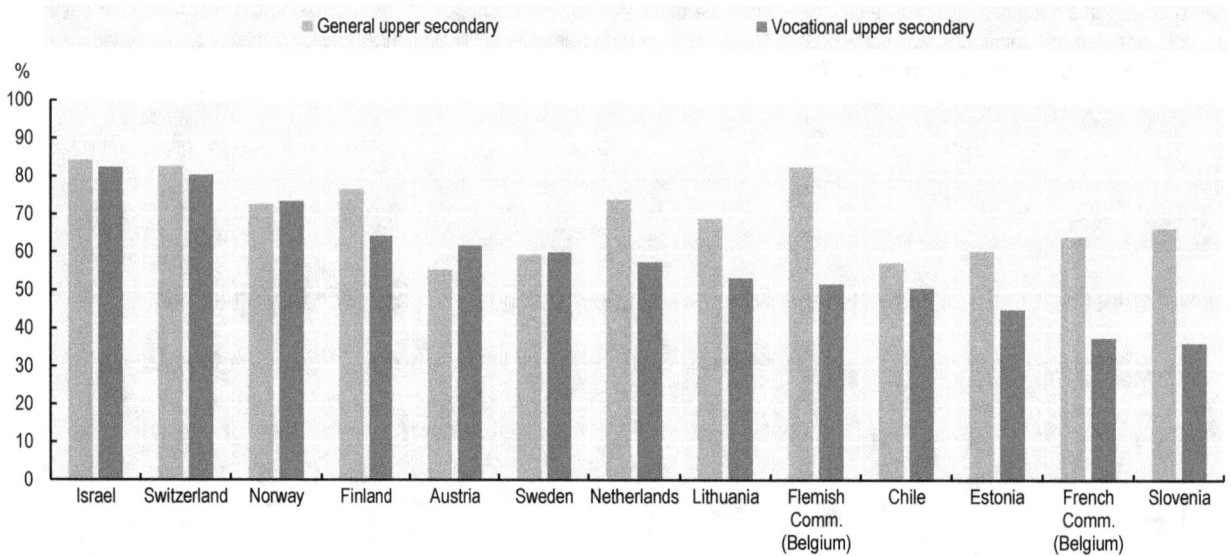

Note: True cohort only.
Source: OECD (2019[10]), *Education at a Glance 2019: OECD Indicators*, https://doi.org/10.1787/f8d7880d-en.

StatLink https://stat.link/oz6r8v

Weaknesses in academic skills, especially literacy and numeracy, are often viewed as a barrier to participation and successful completion in tertiary programmes. Results from the OECD Survey of Adult Skills (PIAAC) show that in many countries a large share of young people leave the upper secondary VET system with weak basic skills (see Figure 2.13). In these countries the share of low literacy performers is also high among young adults with a general upper secondary qualification (and tertiary completion rates tend to be lower too). In almost all countries, the share of young adults with at most an upper-secondary or post-secondary non-tertiary VET who have weak literacy skills is higher than among those with a general qualification at the same level. (In Canada and New Zealand, which are exceptions, the results might be driven by the fact that VET graduates are mostly at ISCED 4, and thus have pursued more education than general upper secondary graduates). This means that successfully engaging VET graduates in tertiary studies requires targeted measures in some countries, such as screening for weaknesses in basic skills and offering remedial courses to those who need it.

Figure 2.13. Share of young people with weak literacy skills, by programme orientation (2012, 2015 or 2017)

16-34 year-olds with upper secondary or postsecondary non tertiary attainment

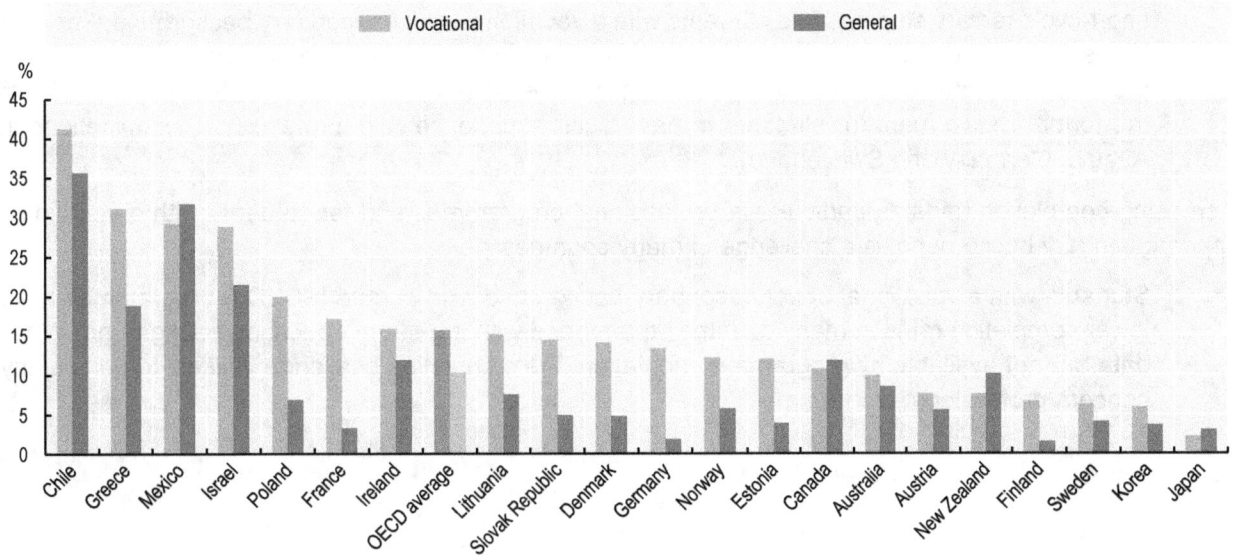

Note: Weak literacy skills are defined here as below level 2. Data refer to 2015 for Chile, Greece, Israel, Lithuania, New Zealand, Slovenia and Turkey. Data refer to 2017 for Hungary, Mexico, and the United States. All other countries refer to 2012.
Source: OECD Survey of Adult Skills (PIAAC), https://www.oecd.org/skills/piaac/

StatLink https://stat.link/yfq4o3

Conclusion

In many countries professional tertiary programmes (including practically-oriented, applied programmes that are designed to play a key role in providing upskilling opportunities for VET graduates.

- In some countries, short-cycle tertiary programmes and bachelor's programmes in UAS-s (or similar institutions with a practical focus) are the only tertiary education option that is directly accessible for upper secondary VET graduates (e.g. in the Netherlands they have direct access to UAS programmes but not regular universities). They also often act as a bridge into the "academic sector" of higher education for upper secondary VET graduates, supporting permeability between the professional and academic sectors of higher education (e.g. in Germany professional tertiary graduates may enter university programmes even if they lack the usually required entrance qualification).
- Some countries have clear options for progression from ISCED 5 to ISCED 6 programmes, typically requiring students to complete 1-2 years of additional education within a related field to obtain a bachelor's level qualification (e.g. top-up programmes for professional academy graduates

in Denmark). But in many cases articulation remains elusive and dependent on decisions by individual institutions.

Cross-sectional data on current tertiary students provide the following insights into progression patterns:

- Most students start tertiary studies directly at ISCED level 6 following their upper secondary education. Short-cycle tertiary programmes are a common entry route into ISCED level 6 in only a handful of countries (e.g. Austria, France, Spain, Sweden).
- In some countries short-cycle tertiary programmes serve mostly upper secondary VET graduates.
- Having some work experience before or during tertiary studies is quite common, particularly among short-cycle tertiary students and students with a vocational upper secondary background. For both levels, pursuing or having past experience in high-skilled occupations is more common among VET graduates. In some countries the high share of work experience in high-skilled occupations reflects the formal requirement for students to have such experience (e.g. professional examinations in Austria, Germany and Switzerland).

Increasing completion rates, in particular in professional programmes and for students with a vocational upper secondary background, is a challenge in many countries:

- Students with a vocational upper secondary background who pursue ISCED 6 programmes have lower completion rates in many countries than those with a general education background. While data are not available by programme orientation, the completion challenge is likely to particularly concern professional programmes.

References

OECD (2021), *OECD Data collection on professional tertiary education*, Unpublished. [7]

OECD (2020), *"Education at a Glance", Education and Training – Education at a Glance (database)*, https://stats.oecd.org/ (accessed on 1 June 2021). [2]

OECD (2020), *2020 INES ad-hoc survey on vocational education and training (VET)*, Unpublished. [11]

OECD (2020), *Education at a Glance 2020: OECD Indicators*, OECD Publishing, Paris, https://doi.org/10.1787/69096873-en. [3]

OECD (2019), *Education at a Glance 2019: OECD Indicators*, OECD Publishing, Paris, https://doi.org/10.1787/f8d7880d-en. [10]

OECD (2014), *Skills Beyond School: Synthesis Report*, OECD Publishing, Paris, http://http//dx.doi.org/10.1787/9789264214682-en. [5]

Onisep (2022), *Les licences professionnelles*, https://www.onisep.fr/Choisir-mes-etudes/Apres-le-bac/Organisation-des-etudes-superieures/Les-licences-professionnelles (accessed on 15 February 2022). [6]

Shapiro, D. et al. (2017), *Tracking Transfer: Measures of Effectiveness in Helping Community College Students to Complete Bachelor's Degrees (Signature Report No.13)*, http://www.luminafoundation.org. (accessed on 29 November 2021). [8]

Statistik Austria (2021), *Studierende, belegte Studien*, https://statistik.at/web_de/statistiken/menschen_und_gesellschaft/bildung/hochschulen/studierende_belegte_studien/index.html (accessed on 2 December 2021). [9]

Ulicna, D., K. Luomi Messerer and M. Auzinger (2016), *Study on higher Vocational Education and Training in the EU*, European Commission, Brussels, https://doi.org/10.2767/421741. [4]

Vandeweyer, M. and A. Verhagen (2020), "The changing labour market for graduates from medium-level vocational education and training", *OECD Social, Employment and Migration Working Papers*, No. 244, OECD Publishing, Paris, https://doi.org/10.1787/503bcecb-en. [1]

3 The profile of learners in professional tertiary programmes

This chapter describes comparative data on the learners who pursue professional tertiary education and training. The age of learners is closely related to the function played by different programmes in skill systems. So where programmes, as in short cycle professional programmes in France, are primarily designed as part of initial education, learners are relatively young, mostly 25 or younger. Where such programmes often serve to upskill adult workers, as in Germany, there are many older learners. Similarly, upskilling short cycle programmes are often delivered part time (as in Switzerland) whereas when the programmes are part of initial education (as in Chile) full-timers dominate. The gender mix in professional programmes is closely related to fields of study: in the field of education, for example, there are more than three times as many women enrolled as men on average in OECD countries.

Introduction

As labour market demand for tertiary education graduates has increased over the past decades, widening access to tertiary education has become a priority in many countries, underpinned by a broader emphasis on social mobility. Programmes with professional orientation are often viewed as a particularly effective means of attracting non-traditional learners – learners who are first in their family to pursue tertiary education, those from lower socio-economic backgrounds or with a migrant background, as well as adult learners. A recent study of higher vocational education and training (VET) in Europe (Ulicna, Luomi Messerer and Auzinger, 2016[1]) highlighted the role of these programmes to serve target groups that are under-represented in tertiary education.

First, the applied and practically-oriented content of programmes is likely to be more appealing to non-traditional learners, especially when the programme is connected to their prior vocational qualification. Second, professional programmes may be easier to access for non-traditional learners. Sometimes the academic entry barriers are lower – for example in Denmark, a system of entry quotas is designed in a way that allows professional programmes to take into account non-academic criteria (e.g. work experience, volunteer work) and assess individually each applicant, while university admissions are mostly driven by grade point average scores (OECD, 2021[2]). For some learners professional programmes are the only easily accessible form of tertiary education. This is the case in countries where graduates of vocational upper secondary programmes have direct access only to professional programmes (or programmes offered in particular types of tertiary education institution) (see Table 2.1 for some examples). Finally, professional programmes are sometimes more affordable. In some countries, tuition fees are lower for short-cycle tertiary programmes than for bachelor's or master's programmes. This is the case, for example, in Korea (OECD, 2021[2]) and the United States, where the average tuition fee for an associate degree in a community college is less than half of that in a four-year institution (NCES, 2021[3]). This makes short-cycle programmes not only an affordable option to obtain a tertiary qualification, but if articulation arrangements exist, also a cheaper route to a bachelor's (or higher level) qualification. In addition, in programmes that are pursued via a dual pathway, learners receive an income while studying, which makes participation more affordable.

As explained earlier, countries were invited through an OECD survey to comment on key challenges in terms of equity as part of the "Data collection on professional tertiary education" conducted for this project. Two equity challenges are commonly highlighted: first, increasing participation and completion among learners from lower socio-economic backgrounds, and second, addressing issues of gender imbalance in some professions. This chapter presents available comparative data on the profile of learners in professional programmes: the age and gender of students, participation in part-time education and some insights into the socio-economic background of students.

Insights from comparative data

The age of students

Figure 3.1 shows the age distribution of current students enrolled in ISCED 5 programmes, illustrating the different functions these programmes play in national skills systems. In Austria, for example, ISCED 5 programmes are in effect a continuation of upper secondary VET (year 4-5 of BHS programmes are classified as level 5 and they follow-up on the first years of upper secondary VET) and are delivered within the same colleges. In Slovenia as well, short-cycle tertiary programmes are delivered within the same centres that provide upper secondary VET and students are mostly young adults. In both Austria and Slovenia a large share of students in ISCED level 5 programmes hold an upper secondary vocational qualification (see Chapter 2). Similarly, in France short-cycle programmes (BTS, BUT or formerly DUT) offer predominantly initial preparation for a first entry into the labour market and enrol young people. But unlike Austria and Slovenia, students less often have a prior vocational qualification – two-thirds of students hold a general upper secondary qualification (see Chapter 2).

Conversely, in countries like Germany, Norway and Sweden adults aged 25 or more represent the majority of short-cycle tertiary students, reflecting a different function played by these programmes. In both Norway and Sweden, programmes of higher vocational education are concentrated at ISCED levels 4 and 5, and are not considered part of the higher education system. Most students in these programmes are aged 25 or more, and build on a relevant vocational qualification and work experience. In Germany master craftsman programmes in trade and technical schools provide upskilling to professionals with an upper secondary vocational qualification and several years of work experience.

Figure 3.1. Age distribution of short-cycle tertiary students (2018)

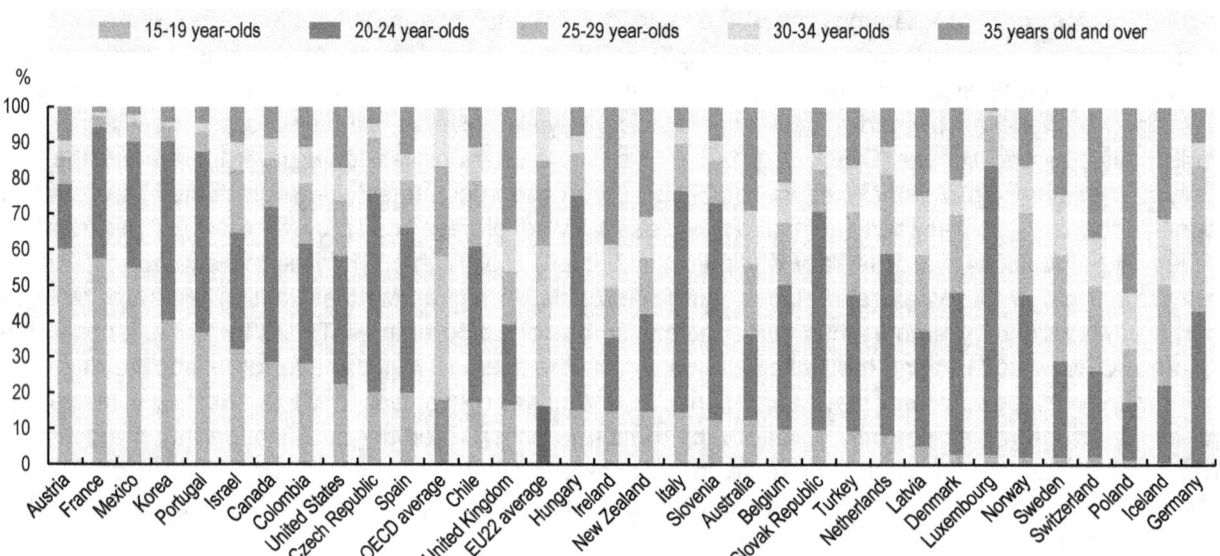

Note: Data for Belgium (French Community) exclude participants in adult higher education.
Source: OECD (2020[4]), "Education at a Glance", Education and Training – Education at a Glance (database), https://stats.oecd.org/.

StatLink https://stat.link/z1yop3

Figure 3.2 shows the age distribution of students enrolled in programmes that are classified by countries as professional at ISCED level 6. In Korea, Belgium, Slovenia, France and Lithuania this category mostly corresponds to "professional bachelor" programmes, which provide initial preparation for a first skilled job and enrol mostly students aged 24 or less. At the other extreme, in Switzerland, Denmark and Germany most students are aged 25 or more. In Switzerland and Germany this reflects the role of professional examinations at this level, which build on several years of work experience and upskill existing professionals.

As illustrated by Figure 3.3, among the countries that chose to distinguish professional from academic programmes, students in professional programmes at ISCED level 6 tend to be older than those pursuing academic programmes (Greece is the only exception). In many countries, the difference is relatively small (one or two years). However, in Denmark and Switzerland that gap is more substantial (six and four years, respectively).

Figure 3.2. Age distribution of professional bachelor's or equivalent students (2018)

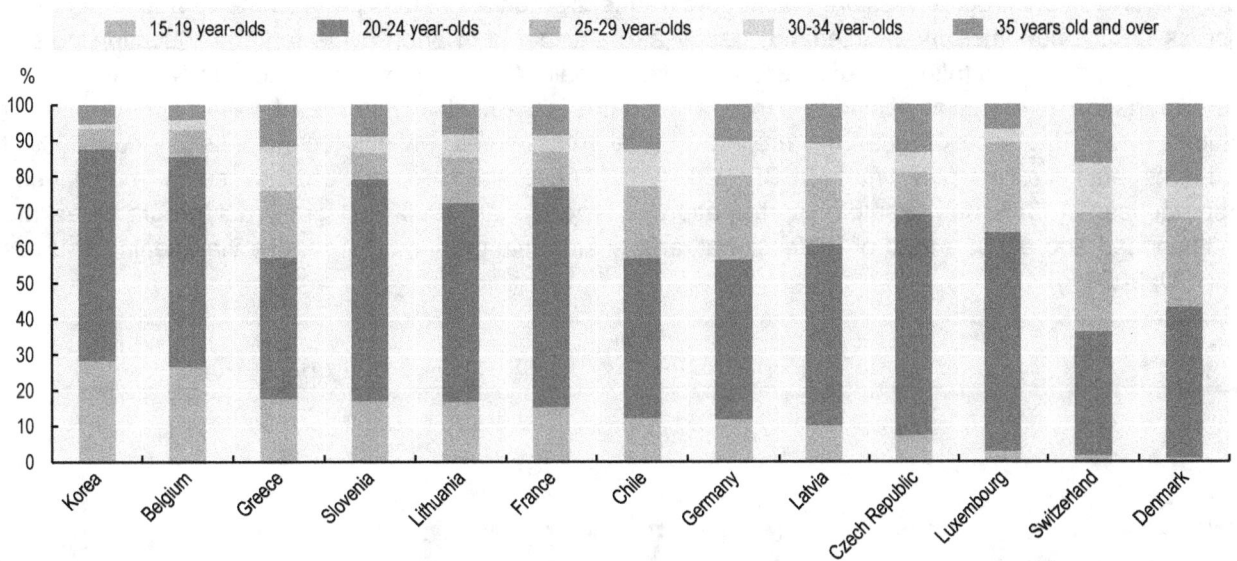

Note: Data are based on national definitions of programme orientation. Data for Belgium (French Community) exclude participants in adult higher education.
Source: OECD (2020[4]), "Education at a Glance", Education and Training – Education at a Glance (database), https://stats.oecd.org/.

StatLink https://stat.link/pv07ah

Figure 3.3. Mean age of students enrolled in bachelor's or equivalent level, by programme orientation (2018)

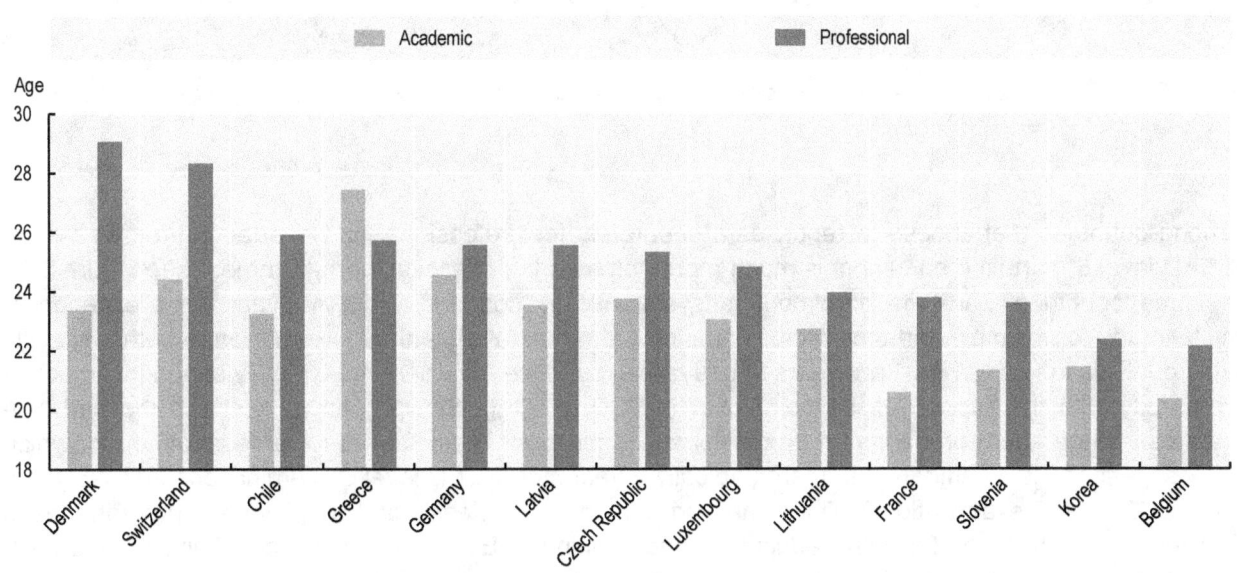

Note: Data are based on national definitions of programme orientation.
Source: OECD (2020[4]), "Education at a Glance", Education and Training – Education at a Glance (database), https://stats.oecd.org/.

StatLink https://stat.link/cf7uxv

Part-time participation

Short-cycle tertiary programmes are much more frequently than bachelor's programmes pursued part time across OECD countries. In Switzerland, nearly all participants in short-cycle tertiary education pursue part-time programmes (although this sector is a very small part of the tertiary sector). In Norway there is some variation across fields of study – almost all students in the fields of health and welfare, primary sector studies and pedagogical programmes are in part-time programmes, while in technical fields about 50% of students are enrolled part time (OECD, 2021[2])). These data do not capture some modularised approaches. In Chile for example, participation is reported as 100% full time, but programmes are modularised and about a third of professional tertiary students pursue their studies via evening courses (CNED, 2021[5])).

Figure 3.4. Share of full-time and part-time students in short-cycle tertiary programmes (2018)

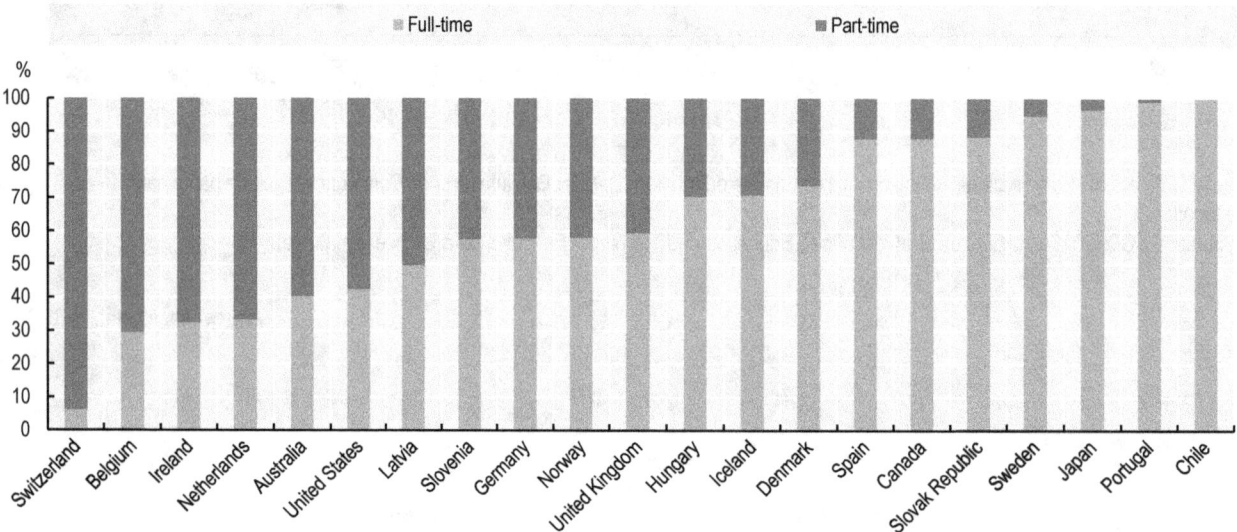

Source: OECD (2020[4]), "Education at a Glance", Education and Training – Education at a Glance (database), https://stats.oecd.org/.

StatLink https://stat.link/5mdrzp

Among countries that choose to report data separately for professional and academic programmes at ISCED level 6, part-time enrolment is much more common in professional programmes (see Figure 3.5). In some countries, part-time enrolment is systematically combined with relevant work experience. In Denmark, for example part-time professional programmes (at all tertiary levels) require both a specific entry qualification and at least two years of relevant experience. Learners are typically experienced adults who study with the support of their employer (OECD, 2021[2]). Similarly, in Switzerland the part-time learners include adults preparing for professional examinations (see Box 1.5 for a description), for which work experience is an entry requirement (typically 2 years for ISCED level 6 examinations and 4-5 years for ISCED level 7 examinations). The remaining students in professional ISCED level 6 programmes in Switzerland study in professional education and training (PET) colleges, which similarly to Danish institutions require relevant work experience for part-time enrolment (OECD, 2021[2]).

Figure 3.5. Share of part-time students in bachelor's or equivalent level, by programme orientation (2018)

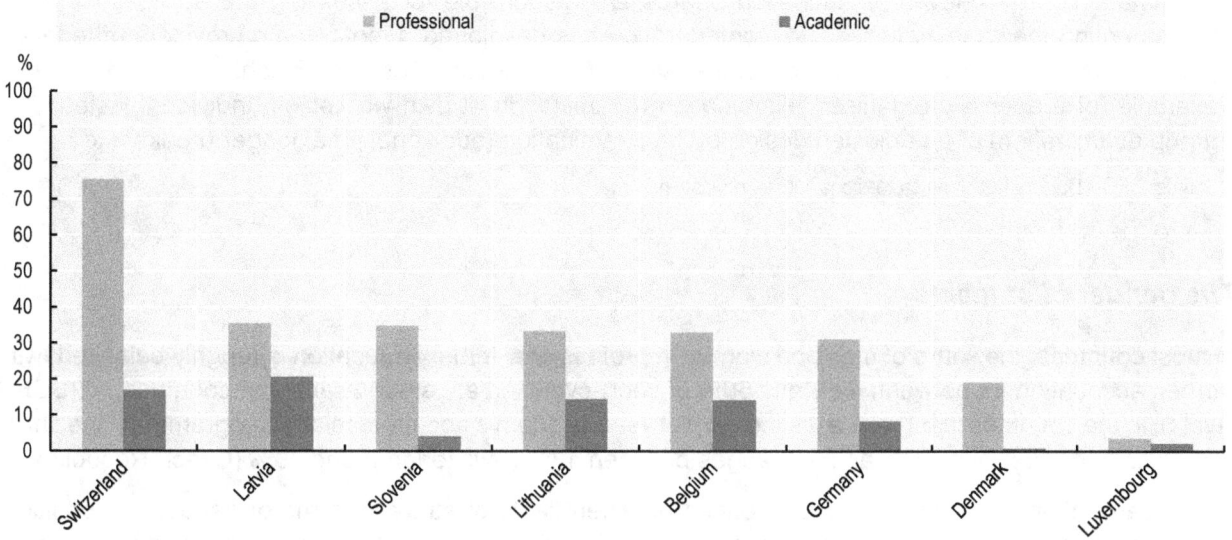

Note: Data are based on national definitions of programme orientation.
Source: OECD (2020[4]), "Education at a Glance", Education and Training – Education at a Glance (database), https://stats.oecd.org/.

StatLink https://stat.link/tfmio0

In answers to the "Data collection on professional tertiary education", many OECD countries reported a common equity framework for both professional and academic tertiary programmes, with similar arrangements in terms of financial support or other targeted measures designed to facilitate access and support completion in tertiary education. In addition to such overarching measures, a number of countries have introduced specific measures to offer flexible learning options within professional programmes – Box 3.1 provides some examples.

> **Box 3.1. Measures to foster inclusion in professional programmes**
>
> **Norway: Increasing access through more flexibility**
>
> Vocational college programmes (ISCED levels 4 and 5) are delivered by a large range of providers, administered and financed at county level. 62% of colleges are private and many are small (47% have less than 50 students). Their offer is highly diverse, ranging from technical and maritime programmes to arts and Bible studies. In technical programmes, most students are male, while there are almost only female students in health and social studies. Most students have some work experience and build on upper secondary education in a technical field, health and welfare. About two-thirds of students pursuing an ISCED level 4 or 5 qualification study part time, as many combine studies with work. A number of measures are designed to increase participation and completion rates, and were combined with increased funding and admission in recent years. These include flexible modes of delivery, such as session-based teaching and part-time education. The regional structure of vocational colleges combined with the option of online learning (almost half of the programmes are partly or completely web-based). Applicants without an upper secondary qualification may be admitted through recognition of prior learning. Audiobooks containing learning material have been introduced to help students with reading or writing difficulties.

Switzerland: Supporting people with disability in professional examinations

People with disabilities can apply for a disadvantage compensation for federal professional examinations. The relevant examination boards are responsible for assessing the applications and implementing the examinations. The Confederation has developed a tool to help providers of federal professional examinations to ensure compensation for disadvantages. This might take the form, for example, of a specially organised examination (examination at own workplace, individual instead of group examination) or an adjusted design of the examination (additional time, longer breaks, etc.).

Source: OECD Data collection on professional tertiary education.

The gender of students

In most countries, the share of men and women in professional tertiary education is roughly balanced, with women accounting for between 40% and 60% of short-cycle tertiary students in most countries. At ISCED level 6, in the countries that make a distinction between academic and professional programmes, the share of women in professional programmes ranges between 43% (Switzerland) and 73% (Czech Republic).

At the same time, there are major differences between fields of study in terms of gender composition. Comparative data are not available on gender by field of study separately for academic and professional programmes. However, as one might expect, data on professional programmes show that in countries where one gender dominates in enrolment, programmes are concentrated in traditionally gender-biased fields of study. For example, Norway has the lowest share of women among short-cycle tertiary students, almost certainly explained by the fact that 62% of graduates at this level completed a programme in the field of engineering, manufacturing and construction. In Poland, the opposite holds: 84% of students are women and all programmes at this level are in the field of health and welfare (see Chapter 4).

Figure 3.6. Share of women enrolled in short-cycle tertiary and in professional ISCED level 6 programmes (2018)

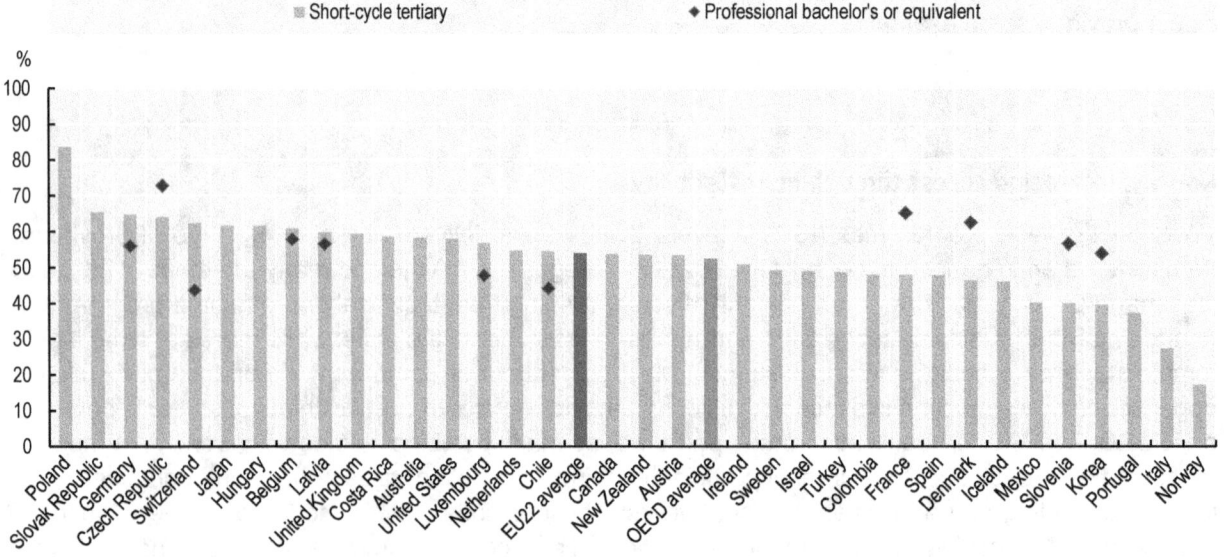

Note: Data for short-cycle tertiary education is for all programme orientations. Data for ISCED level 6 programmes are based on national definitions of programme orientation.
Source: OECD (2020[4]), "Education at a Glance", Education and Training – Education at a Glance (database), https://stats.oecd.org/.

StatLink https://stat.link/n0yg31

In the absence of comparative data by programme orientation and field of study, Figure 3.7 shows the gender balance in some selected fields of study, which may be considered sector- or profession-oriented. Women are strongly over-represented at the tertiary education level in fields such as education and health and welfare, and men in the fields of information and communication technologies (ICT) and engineering. Only three out of nine fields of study have a balanced gender distribution on average across countries: Services, "Agriculture, forestry, fisheries and veterinary" and "Business, administration and law".

Figure 3.7. Share of women enrolled in selected fields of study (2018)

OECD average, all tertiary education levels

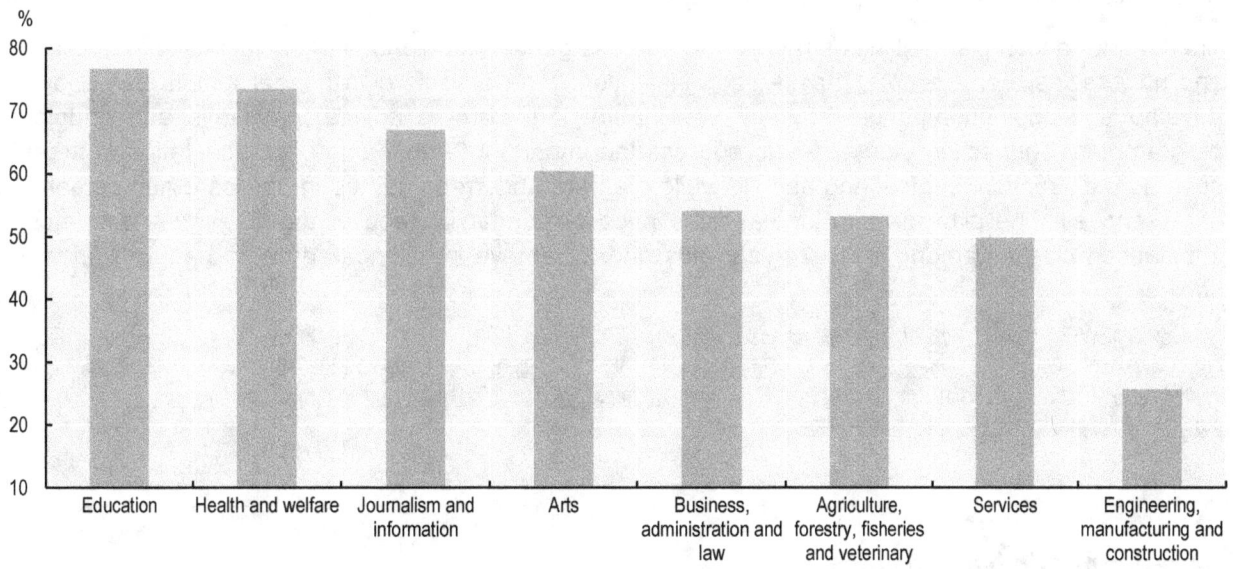

Source: OECD (2020[4]), "Education at a Glance", Education and Training – Education at a Glance (database), https://stats.oecd.org/.

StatLink https://stat.link/9vnspm

Gender segregation by field of study is linked to the gender pay gap. Among tertiary students, men tend to dominate the fields that yield the best employment prospects in terms of wages, such as ICT or engineering, manufacturing and construction, while women account for the majority of students in lower paid fields such as education or health and welfare (see Figure 4.4 for relevant data for ISCED level 5 programmes). Making sure that well-paid sectors such as ICT and engineering are reflected in training programmes which are attractive to women might play a part in reducing the gender pay gap.

International evidence shows that the lower engagement of women in science, technology, engineering, and mathematics (STEM) fields of study is not driven by academic performance in science – the overall performance of girls and boys in science at age 15 is similar across different countries, but girls are likely to be even better at reading and choose based on their "comparative" (rather than "absolute") strengths (Mostafa, 2019[6]). An overview of research (Kahn and Ginther, 2017[7]) shows that the gender STEM gap is driven by gendered stereotypes, culture, role models, competition, risk aversion and interests. These differences start at childhood and affects children and young adults as they progress through their education and into the labour market.

In response to the strongly biased participation patterns in different fields of study, several countries have introduced initiatives designed to attract women to traditionally male occupations and vice versa. Box 3.2 provides some examples.

> **Box 3.2. Initiatives to reduce the gender imbalance in professional programmes**
>
> **Girls' Day – Future for girls day – Daughter's day in Austria**
>
> A wide range of initiatives, with different names are implemented with a common objective: bring girls closer to the world of work, especially male-dominated occupations, widening career options and study choices. Girls have a day off school and participate in different activities, such as getting a taste of some occupations (e.g. programming computers, or repairing cars), or visiting companies to learn about occupations involved.
>
> **Gender action plan in Scotland (United Kingdom)**
>
> The Gender action plan outlines strategies to address gender imbalances at subject level in colleges and universities. For example, it asks each institution to develop its own gender action plan and to develop a school engagement strategy seeking to offer careers advice, pathways and bridging programmes. This action plan seeks to address the important female under-representation in areas such as construction, engineering and IT, while men are underrepresented in childcare and personal care services. The plan aims to increase the minority gender in each of the 10 largest and most imbalanced classes among 16-to 24-year-olds and to remove imbalances greater than 75% in any subject.
>
> Source: BMBWF (2022[8]), *Girls' Day - MädchenZukunftstag – Töchtertag* [Girls' Day – Girls' Future Day – Daughters' Day], https://www.bmbwf.gv.at/Themen/schule/schulpraxis/ba/gs/geschlechtss_bo/girlsday.html; Cedefop (2020[9]), *Developments in vocational education and training policy in 2015-19: UK Scotland*, https://www.cedefop.europa.eu/en/publications-and-resources/country-reports/developments-vocational-education-and-training-policy-2015-19-uk-scotland.

Socio-economic background

Comparative data on the socio-economic background of students in professional programmes are limited, as relevant data are not collected as part of regular data collections that distinguish by programme orientation. Even at national level data appear to be scarce – a European study of short-cycle tertiary education (Kirsch and Beernaert, 2011[10]) found that while there was a widely held view among ministries and providers across different countries that short-cycle tertiary programmes contribute to widening participation in higher education and promoting social cohesion, relevant data in support of this proposition were rarely available. Figure 3.8 provides some insights based on the Survey of Adult Skills, a product of the Programme for the International Assessment of Adult Competencies (PIAAC). Professional programmes appear to play an important role in allowing individuals to acquire a tertiary qualification first in their family. The share of adults with at least one tertiary-educated parent is lower among short-cycle tertiary graduates than among adults holding a bachelor's degree or equivalent in all but two countries (and in those countries the difference is very small).

Figure 3.8. Share of tertiary graduates with at least one tertiary-educated parent

Adults aged 25-64 with tertiary attainment, by type of tertiary qualification

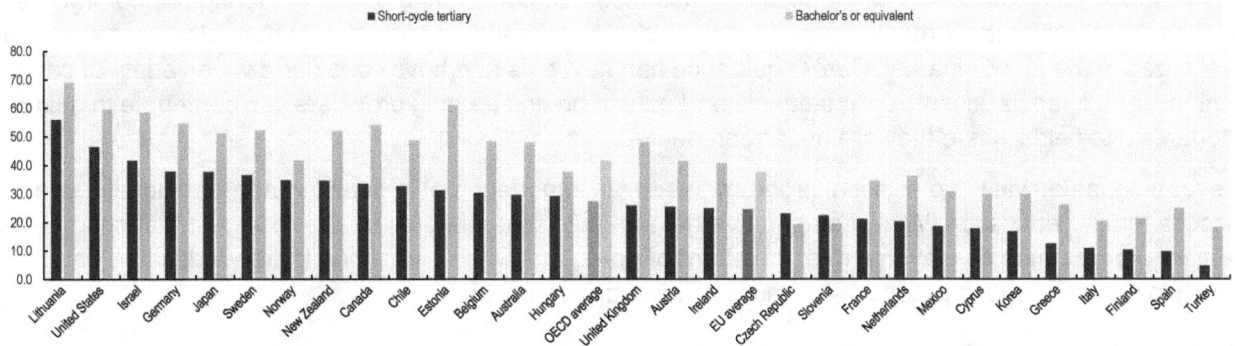

Note: Data refer to 2015 for Chile, Greece, Israel, Lithuania, New Zealand, Slovenia and Turkey. Data refer to 2017 for Hungary and the United States. All other countries refer to 2012. The Survey of Adult Skills (PIAAC) is based on ISCED-97. The labels in this chart have been adapted so that they refer to the closest equivalents: Short-cycle tertiary education = ISCED-97 5B, Bachelor's or equivalent = ISCED-97 5A.
Source: OECD Survey of Adult Skills (PIAAC), https://www.oecd.org/skills/piaac/.

StatLink https://stat.link/3gba74

Conclusion

Countries differ strongly in terms of the age distribution of students in professional tertiary education programmes. Variation regarding the age of students, as well as the use of part-time participation, both across countries and between programmes within individual countries, illustrates the different functions professional programmes play in national skills systems.

Younger adults dominate in programmes providing initial preparation for labour market entry. Programmes are designed to equip recent upper secondary graduates of with occupational skills. Short-cycle tertiary programmes in Austria, Slovenia, France and Italy usually play this role. Similarly, professional bachelor's programmes across various European countries (e.g. Belgium, Lithuania, Slovenia, France) tend to enrol young adults and prepare them for a first skilled job.

Older adults dominate in programmes offering other functions, including:

- Upskilling for existing professionals: Programmes build on a relevant prior vocational qualification and several years of relevant work experience. Students often combine studies with employment in a relevant sector. For example, professional examinations in Germany and Switzerland often have this function.
- Reskilling for adults: Programmes are used to support a career shift. While students may have work experience and work part-time, their employment is not necessarily related to the targeted field of study. A programme may serve as a tool for reskilling if it does not require relevant work experience – instead participants may obtain such experience during their studies through work-based learning. For example, in Denmark professional programmes may be pursued full time (with an internship) or part time for those with relevant work experience.

Countries that want to make their programmes more accessible to adult learners, may need to increase the flexibility of their professional programmes, including in terms of part-time options, recognition of prior learning and modularisation.

The gender balances in professional tertiary education also differs strongly between countries, and largely reflects the fields-of-study of the professional programmes on offer. Female students are predominantly enrolled in fields such as, health and social care and teaching. By contrast, male students are much more likely than female students to be enrolled in construction, manufacturing and engineering programmes, as well as IT programmes. Breaking gender stereotypes is crucial, and can contribute to closing the gender wage gap in the labour market. Career guidance can help girls and boys consider a wide variety of career options, and financial incentives to students and education and training providers can contribute to guiding students into fields where they are underrepresented.

Several countries view professional programmes as an important tool in enabling non-traditional students access tertiary education. While comparative data on this issue are limited, they suggest that short-cycle tertiary programmes do play that role: the share of graduates with at least one tertiary-educated parent is much lower than among graduates of bachelor-level programmes.

References

BMBWF (2022), *Girls' Day - MädchenZukunftstag - Töchtertag*, https://www.bmbwf.gv.at/Themen/schule/schulpraxis/ba/gs/geschlechtss_bo/girlsday.html (accessed on 15 February 2022). [8]

Cedefop (2020), "Developments in vocational education and training policy in 2015-19: UK Scotland", *Cedefop monitoring and analysis of VET policies.*, https://www.cedefop.europa.eu/en/publications-and-resources/country-reports/developments-vocational-education-and-training-policy-2015-19-uk-scotland (accessed on 28 February 2022). [9]

CNED (2021), *Consejo Nacional de Educación. Indices Educación Superior*, https://www.cned.cl/indices/matricula-sistema-de-educacion-superior (accessed on 22 December 2021). [5]

Kahn, S. and D. Ginther (2017), "Women and STEM", *NBER Working Paper Series* 23525, https://doi.org/10.3386/W23525. [7]

Kirsch, M. and Y. Beernaert (2011), *Short Cycle Higher Education in Europe. Level 5: the Missing Link*, EURASHE, Brussels. [10]

Mostafa, T. (2019), "Why don't more girls choose to pursue a science career?", *PISA in Focus*, No. 93, OECD Publishing, Paris, https://doi.org/10.1787/02bd2b68-en. [6]

NCES (2021), *Fast Facts: Tuition costs of colleges and universities*, https://nces.ed.gov/fastfacts/display.asp?id=76 (accessed on 30 November 2021). [3]

OECD (2021), *OECD Data collection on professional tertiary education*, Unpublished. [2]

OECD (2020), *"Education at a Glance", Education and Training – Education at a Glance (database)*, https://stats.oecd.org/ (accessed on 1 June 2021). [4]

Ulicna, D., K. Luomi Messerer and M. Auzinger (2016), *Study on higher Vocational Education and Training in the EU*, European Commission, Brussels, https://doi.org/10.2767/421741. [1]

4 Ensuring the relevance of professional tertiary programmes

To be of value, professional programmes need to develop the skills needed by the labour market. This chapter looks at some evidence and indicators showing how well that is achieved in practice. Work-based learning plays a critical role, both because it provides a powerful learning environment in which students may acquire the hard and soft skills needed in the workplace, and because it offers a framework in which employers and potential recruits may get to know one another, facilitating transition to employment. This chapter reports some new evidence on the use of work placements in professional tertiary education, especially on the extent to which such placements are mandatory. In addition, this chapter describes the institutional architecture which facilitates engagement of professional tertiary education with the world of work. It also provides data on the different fields of study included within professional tertiary education and their links to subsequent labour market outcomes.

Introduction

Close connections with the world of work are important for all tertiary programmes, especially for programmes with professional orientation. A series of case studies of professional tertiary education in Europe found that strong links with social partners represents one of the strengths of this sector. Strong employer engagement appears to be facilitated by looser regulation compared to upper secondary vocational education and training (VET), making it easier to adapt provision to changing needs, and employer interest in the type of skills provided by this sector (Ulicna, Luomi Messerer and Auzinger, 2016[1]). The first section of this chapter focuses on how countries create linkages between professional programmes and the world of work. It looks at the institutional framework underpinning employer engagement at national, sectoral, regional and institutional levels. Work-based learning receives specific attention in this chapter, because it is a powerful way of connecting education and training programmes with the world of work, and comparative data and information provide rich insights.

Workplaces provide a strong learning environment for the acquisition of both technical skills and generic employability skills, as students learn from real life problems and from professionals familiar with the latest technologies and working methods. Employers benefit from the productive work of students and can save on costly recruitment selection, as they can observe students, as potential recruits, at work and skip much of the initial training that external recruits need (Muehlemann and Leiser, 2015[2]). When work-based learning is mandatory, provider institutions must develop partnerships with employers. This gives employers valuable influence over the mix of programmes provided, ensuring that students pursue training that is in demand in the labour market and that public funding for skills development is shaped by labour market needs. Work-based learning is also value for money for providers and public authorities: it reduces the cost of delivery, particularly in fields where modern equipment is expensive and needs frequent updating, and where recruiting professionals familiar with the latest techniques is hard and costly (OECD, 2014[3]).

Recognising the compelling advantaged of work-based learning, various recent European declarations and policy documents have called for the development of work-based learning in education and training programmes. These continue the process of enhancing European cooperation in VET, setting out priorities, targets and deliverables. The Bruges Communiqué (2010) set out objectives and actions to enhance the quality of VET, making it more accessible and responsive to labour market needs. The Riga Conclusions, endorsed by European ministers in 2015, included medium-term deliverables designed to raise the quality and status of VET. One of five priority areas was the promotion of work-based learning in all its forms, with special attention to apprenticeships. More recently, the Osnabrück declaration (2020), focused on recovery and transitions to digital and green economies, included the reinforcement of work-based learning and apprenticeships among the deliverables for 2021-2025. In line with this, the 2020 Council Recommendation on VET for sustainable competitiveness, social fairness and resilience includes some specific targets: it encourages countries to work towards ensuring that by 2025, 60% of recent VET graduates benefit from work-based learning during their vocational programme. It highlights the need to include work-based learning in vocational programmes at all levels and further develop apprenticeship schemes, with appropriate support measures and incentives to encourage employer engagement.

The development of work-based learning has been highlighted as one of the main trends shaping the professional tertiary landscape in Europe (Ulicna, Luomi Messerer and Auzinger, 2016[1]). Yet various barriers mean that not all professional programmes make effective use of work-based learning. For employers providing high-quality work-based learning is demanding, requiring the capacity to manage partially skilled workers and integrate them into work processes, as well as dealing with the associated administrative burden. There are often barriers on the education provider side too, as integrating work-based learning into programmes requires a different organisation of the learning process and different ways of assessing learning outcomes. As a result of these barriers, work placements are sometimes optional additions to programmes or lack quality assurance.

The mix of provision – meaning the fields of study, programmes within fields of study and the number of students within those programmes, needs to reflect various factors. It should take into account immediate labour market needs to allow for smooth transitions into jobs, as well as expected long-term developments so that graduates can have successful careers. Yet often the mix of provision is driven by constraints of provider institutions and student choice that is often not sufficiently informed. Data availability on the mix of provision delivered by professional programmes across OECD countries is very limited. Data by highly aggregated categories of field of study are available only at short-cycle level, giving an indication of the breadth of this sector in different countries, complementing enrolment data which are indicative of their size. At ISCED level 6, countries do not provide data by field of study and programme orientation – and if data were to be collected, they would need to be based on internationally agreed definitions to add real value.

Knowing what graduates of different education and training programmes do upon graduation and the careers they pursue provides crucial feedback on skills systems and informs efforts to improve them. Recognising this, in the 2017 Council Recommendation, European Union Member States made a commitment to collect data on graduates from higher education and VET in a way that allows for international comparisons and benchmarking. The final section of this chapter provides insights on outcomes from different types of tertiary programmes. Given data availability constraints, the analysis primarily concerns short-cycle tertiary education (or programmes that are close equivalents) and provides data on ISCED level 6 programmes as a point of comparison. The analysis explores outcomes in terms of employment rates and earnings, and provides some insights on the basic skills of graduates and work strain as an indicator of job quality.

Insights from comparative data

This section first examines how countries build connections between professional tertiary programmes and the world of work: frameworks for employer engagement and the use of work-based learning in professional programmes. It then looks at the different fields of study within short-cycle tertiary programmes and ISCED level 6 programmes regardless of orientation (it is not possible to break down data by programme orientation at level 6). Finally, it explores employment outcomes associated with professional tertiary education.

Links with the world of work

Employer engagement

The institutional framework underpinning employer engagement typically includes bodies at national and regional level (sometimes involving different bodies for different economic sectors) and/or at the level of individual institutions. At national (or sectoral) level, advisory committees commonly include social partners and provide strategic guidance regarding policy development and implementation in the light of skills needs. Examples include the Advisory Council for Technical Professional Training in Chile, the Assembly of Councillors of state-owned higher education institutions in Estonia, National Professional Advisory Commissions in France, the National Council of Vocational College Education in Norway, the Council for Vocational and Professional Education in Slovenia, and the General Council for VET and Regional Councils for VET in Spain. Several countries also require individual institutions to have systematic engagement with employers through institutional education boards or committees. For example, in France employers are members of higher education institution boards, in Denmark each provider institution is required to have employer panels or education committees with labour market knowledge and in Estonia institutions must include employers in the committees associated with each study programme.

Primarily at national level, but also sometimes regionally, most countries report systematic involvement of social partners in the development and updating of programmes and curricula, through their involvement in advisory bodies such as those set out above and/or accreditation criteria, which require support from social partners for the proposed programmes and curricula. For example, in the Czech Republic the Accreditation Commission for Tertiary Professional Education includes representatives of the world of work and in Luxembourg accreditation committees are composed of 50% national experts or professionals and 50% international experts in quality assurance.

At a more local level, employers and practising professionals also often play an important role in the delivery of professional programmes. Several countries report that professionals often work as regular teaching staff or guest lecturers (e.g. France, Israel, Italy, Luxembourg, Norway). Spain has a specific category of teaching staff, "specialist teachers": these are experienced practitioners who completed some pedagogical training and teach certain modules part-time. In addition, Spain also encourages teachers to regularly pursue job-shadowing for short periods of time to update their technical skills. More directly, employers may also deliver training themselves through work-based learning, when they host interns or apprentices. They may also support their employees (financially and/or by granting them release from work) who pursue part-time programmes. The use of work-based learning is discussed in detail in the following section.

Finally, in some countries industry representatives take an active role in the design and delivery of final assessments. Their engagement is fundamental in professional examinations – in Switzerland, employers are involved through their professional organisations, which set up examination regulations and employers participate in examinations as examiners. In other types of professional programmes (not professional examinations), industry representatives are less often involved. In Italy, they are systematically engaged, as the final assessments of ITS courses are led by examination boards that include experts from the world of work. In addition, a few other countries report that employers may participate in assessments – such as in examination boards in tertiary professional programmes in the Czech Republic.

Box 4.1 provides some country examples of how social partners are engaged in the design and delivery of professional programmes.

> **Box 4.1. Employer engagement in professional programmes**
>
> **Denmark**
>
> Employers and/or labour market organisations participate in the design of programmes. They are also involved at the stage when provider institutions submit applications to the ministry for new programmes, as applications must include documentation of labour market relevance. In addition, institutions are required to have employer panels or education committees with labour market knowledge, and involve them in the development of existing and new programmes. Employers are also directly involved in programmes through the mandatory internships.
>
> **Estonia**
>
> Employer representatives are included in the assembly of councillors of state-owned professional higher education institutions. The assembly of councillors is an advisory body that makes proposals to the rector, the council and the ministry regarding the development of the institution. When HEIs apply to start providing a new programme, they need to justify why the programme is needed, including arguments advanced by relevant professional associations. In addition, each study programme has an associated committee, which includes employer representatives. Upon registration of study programme in Education Information System by the Ministry of Education and Research, the employer's contribution is also described in the study-programme documentation.

France

National professional advisory commissions (11 in total, for different sectors) oversee the introduction, updating or removal of state-recognised professional qualifications. They are part of "France Compétences", which identifies skills needs and supports the development of high-quality and efficient models of delivery. In addition, employers are members of the boards of higher education institutions. In the delivery of programmes, experienced professionals are present as teachers, joint projects based on a contract between students and a company are commonly used and work-based learning is systematic, with many institutions having partnerships with employers to secure placements for interns or apprentices.

Italy

Courses in higher technical institutes (ITS) are co-designed with companies. The final assessments are conducted by examination boards, composed of representatives of the school, university, professional training, and experts from the world of work. The provider institutions through the regional coordination Committees analyse the job requests of the regional territory and then plan the training offer. The final exam must include the presentation (written and / or oral) of the resolution of a problem faced during the internship activities which demonstrates the student's ability to apply the knowledge acquired during the course of study, under the supervision of one or more internal lecturers who can also be accompanied by external professional or corporate experts.

Source: OECD Data collection on professional tertiary education.

Work-based learning

The following paragraphs examine how work-based learning is used in professional programmes. Work-based learning is understood here as "some combination of observing, undertaking and reflecting on productive work in real workplaces" (OECD, 2017[4]), the definition used in ISCED mappings and the UOE and LSO data collections. Crucially, this definition excludes practical training in simulated work environments such as workshops within provider institutions. Table 4.1 focuses on ISCED level 5 programmes and Table 4.2 on ISCED level 6 programmes that countries currently classify as professional (for programmes classified as "academic" all but one country reported no systematic inclusion of work-based learning in the "Data collection on professional tertiary education"). The tables refer to work-based learning that accounts for at least 25% of programme duration, because this threshold is used in comparative data collections (programmes containing 25-90% work-based learning are considered "combined school and work-based programmes, otherwise they are considered school-based or work-based). Smaller work-based learning components are described under "additional information" in the tables.

In short-cycle tertiary education work-based learning is very common, either a mandatory component for all students, or more selectively, in some programmes and for some of the students (see Table 4.1). Several countries have made work-based learning mandatory for all students and specify its minimum duration: associate degrees in Belgium (both French and Flemish community), academy professional programmes in Denmark, BTS and DUT programmes in France, higher technical institutes in Italy, BTS programmes in Luxembourg, CteSP courses Portugal, short-cycle programmes in Slovenia and higher VET in Spain. Several other countries report that work-based learning is used in short-cycle tertiary programmes, but not necessarily in all programmes and by all provider institutions.

Table 4.1. The use of work-based learning in short-cycle tertiary education

	Includes at least 25% of work-based learning	Additional information
Australia	Yes	Vocational education and training often requires practical elements, including structured workplace learning, as part of the course curriculum.
Austria	No	Practical experience is provided through visits to firms, training in school workshops, training in firms and compulsory summer internships.
Belgium (French Comm.)	Yes	Associate degree programmes include a mandatory traineeship, which accounts for at last 1/3 of the programme.
Belgium (Flanders)	Yes	Associate degree programmes include mandatory work-based learning that accounts for at least 1/3 of the programme (seven months).
Canada	Not all programmes/ students	Work-based learning is a feature of all professional education programmes, but there is variation in its form depending on professional requirements and the design of individual programmes.
Chile	Not all programmes/ students	Higher technical education and professional higher education includes combined school and work-based learning options, but participation in work-based learning is optional.
Colombia	No	
Czech Republic	No	Minimum two weeks of the art practice and at minimum 30 lessons of art teaching practice must be included in the school education programmes.
Denmark	Yes	Internships are compulsory in full-time academy professions programmes. In part-time programmes there is no work placement but relevant work experience is an entry requirement and programme build on it.
England (United Kingdom)	Not all programmes/ students	
France	Yes	DUT and BTS programmes include a mandatory internship (16 weeks), or may be pursued via a work-study pathway alternating school-based and work-based periods.
Germany	Yes	Master craftsman programmes are attended after several years of work experience, which account for about 60% of programme duration.
Israel	Not all programmes/ students	Students may either pursue an apprenticeship or mainly school-based studies with exposure to the industry (e.g. work placement, graduation project carried out in industry).
Italy	Yes	Traineeships are mandatory and account for 30% of programme duration.
Japan	No	About one-third of graduation credits are obtained through practical training, half of which must take place in companies.
Korea	No	The use work-based learning varies across majors and provider institutions, but does not exceed 25% of the curriculum.
Latvia	No	Practical training is compulsory, but work-based learning options are not offered at ISCED level 5 yet.
Luxembourg	Yes	Programmes include at least 228 hours of internship in a professional environment. The minimum length and organisation varies: internships can constitute a whole module or can be part of a module, may be organised in one or several blocks, spread throughout the programme or take place at the end.
Mexico	No	
Netherlands	No	A small share of students pursue combined school and work-based learning programmes.
New Zealand	Not all programmes/ students	The extent to which work based learning is used in professional tertiary education varies across programmes and providers.
Norway	Yes	Higher vocational college education is principally school-based and with an increasing element of web-based learning. Session-based teaching opens for inclusion of work-based learning. Most students are, however, also in relevant employment.
Poland	No	

	Includes at least 25% of work-based learning	Additional information
Portugal	Yes	Programmes include an internship, which takes at least one semester. Additional practical training is included in the technical component of programmes (in laboratories, workshops, and through projects).
Slovak Republic	Yes	
Slovenia	Yes	Programmes are intertwined with work in a working environment. Students must pursue practical training with an employer for at least 10 weeks per year (so 20 weeks in total).
Spain	Not all programmes/ students	All higher VET programmes include a mandatory work placement module of 400 hours / 3 months. Students pursuing dual VET spend over 34% of their programme in work-based learning. Students with previous related work experience may be exempt.
Sweden	Yes (most programmes)	Higher VET programmes leading to an advanced higher VET diploma, include mandatory work-based learning, which accounts for at least 25% of programme duration. Most other higher VET programmes include work-based learning, even though it is not formally required.
Switzerland	No	These programmes not subject to federal regulation.
Turkey	Yes	Work-based learning is mandatory and may take different forms: some postsecondary VET schools offer programmes with 50% at school and 50% in the workplace, while some follow a 3+1 model with one semester in the workplace.

Source: OECD Data collection on professional tertiary education.

The use of mandatory work-based learning is less common in programmes classified as "professional" at ISCED level 6 than in ISCED level 5 programmes (see Table 4.2). Work-based learning is systematically used in professional bachelor's programmes in Denmark, bachelor of technology or professional bachelor's programmes in France (which may also be pursued through dual training), professional examinations in Germany, professional examinations and professional education and training (PET) colleges in Switzerland, professional higher education in Slovenia (though its duration may account for less than 25%) and higher VET in Spain. Many countries report using work-based learning but not for all students, with some variation across programmes and provider institutions.

Table 4.2. The use of work-based learning in professional programmes at ISCED level 6

	Includes at least 25% of work-based learning	Additional comments
OECD		
Belgium (French comm.)	No	Work-based learning is a mandatory component for some programmes, but may account for less than 25% of the programme duration.
Belgium (Flanders)	Noz	The institutions of higher education are free to choose their teaching methods and tools.
Canada	Not all programmes/ students	Variation depending on professional requirements and the design of individual programmes. Work-based learning is a feature of all professional education programmes.
Chile	Not all programmes/ students	Professional higher education (non academic degree-granting) includes work-based learning but not for all students. It is mandatory only if the study plan for the provider institution stipulates it. Medical or dental specialisation programmes include different types of work-based learning.
Czech Republic	Yes	Professionally-oriented bachelor's programmes include work practice of at least 12 weeks.
Denmark	Yes	Approximately 25% of the duration of the programme consists of internships.
France	Yes	Bachelor of technology include a compulsory internship (22 to 26 weeks over 3 years), as do professional bachelor's programmes (12 to 16 weeks over one year)

	Includes at least 25% of work-based learning	Additional comments
Germany	Yes	Master craftsman programmes are attended after several years of work experience, which is required to pass the final examination.
Japan	Yes	About one-third of graduation credits are obtained through practical training, half of which must take place in companies.
Korea	Not all programmes/ students	In some fields, work-based training takes about 2 to 4 weeks.
Latvia	No	Work-based learning is used mostly in medicine and dentistry.
Lithuania	Yes	Work-based learning is increasingly used. Practical training with an employer is mandatory in colleges and accounts for 30 ECTS.
Netherlands	No	A small share of students pursue combined school and work-based learning programmes.
Slovenia	No	Work-based learning is a mandatory component of professional higher education, but may account for less than 25% of the programme duration.
Switzerland	Yes	The combination of professional practice and classroom instruction depends on the type of programme, ranging from mostly work-based learning with some preparatory courses (professional examinations) to full-time education in PET colleges combined with internships.
Partner		
Brazil	Not all programmes/ students	Some programmes include mandatory internships.

Source: OECD Data collection on professional tertiary education.

Work-based learning in professional programmes may take different forms, including internships, dual tertiary programmes and past or ongoing work experience as a form of work-based learning. Internships (understood here as work placements of several weeks or months) are commonly used in professional programmes, although they are sometimes shorter than 25% of programme duration – students in BHS programme in Austria must complete summer internships, in Denmark full-time students in professional academy programmes or professional bachelor's programmes must complete an internship. In France both short-cycle tertiary programmes and bachelor's level programmes include a mandatory internship with minimum duration defined in national legislation, or else may be pursued through dual training (see Box 4.2). In Italy, both higher technical institute (ITS) courses and professionally-oriented degrees (LP) include mandatory internships. In Portugal, two-year vocational and technical higher education courses (CTeSP) include at least a one-semester internship. In programmes that engage both students seeking an initial qualification and experienced adults, countries often allow for some flexibility. For example, in Denmark those with relevant work experience might pursue their professional bachelor's programme part time and without an internship, while those studying full-time must complete an internship. Similarly, in Spain, all higher VET programmes include a compulsory work placement, but students with relevant work experience are granted exemption.

Dual tertiary programmes are also increasingly common across OECD countries, although the nomenclature varies from one country to another. They include, for example, dual UAS programmes in Austria, *Master en Alternance* in Belgium (French Community), *alternance* arrangements in France, dual higher education in Hungary, dual higher VET in Spain, degree apprenticeships in England (United Kingdom) and graduate apprenticeships in Scotland (United Kingdom). However, not all dual tertiary programmes are classified as "professional" by countries in comparative data collections. A recent study of higher VET in the European Union (EU) (Ulicna, Luomi Messerer and Auzinger, 2016[1]) noted that these programmes may be included in a broad definition of "higher VET" but not in a narrow definition – among the examples included in Box 4.2, only France classifies dual programmes as professional in comparative data collections.

> ### Box 4.2. Dual tertiary programmes
>
> **France**
>
> A wide range of programmes may be pursued via a dual pathway (alternance), including ISCED 5 professional qualifications (e.g. BTS, DUT) and ISCED 6 qualifications (e.g. professional bachelor). Students sign an "apprenticeship contract" and obtain a formal educational qualification upon completion. This contract targets mainly 16-29 year-olds, though those aged 30 or more may also sign an apprenticeship contract in special cases. The contract usually covers one to three years and off-the-job training accounts for at least 25% of the contract duration. "Professionalisation contracts" cover dual training that leads to a recognised professional qualification (not a formal educational qualification). They target students aged 16-25 (or above 26 for job seekers) and usually cover 6-12 months, with off-the-job training accounting for minimum 150 hours and 15-25% of the contract duration.
>
> **Germany**
>
> Dual study programmes combine a university course (provided by a university, UAS or vocational academy) and company-based practical experience. They are delivered either through alternating blocks of several weeks or months, or alternating days within a week. Programmes are available in business and administration, civil, industrial or mechanical engineering, tourism management, social work and care management. There are three different forms of the programme. **Dual studies with VET** take 4.5 years to complete and yield a university degree and a vocational qualification. **Dual studies with practical training** put stronger emphasis on practical training and lead to a university degree (but no vocational qualification). **Job-integrating dual studies** offer professional development to those who already hold a vocational or professional qualification, or have professional experience, even if they lack the usually required entrance qualification. Students' coursework is based on a contract signed between their employer, the UAS and the student.
>
> **Scotland (United Kingdom)**
>
> The Graduate Apprenticeship scheme, launched in 2017/18, is delivered in co-operation with selected universities in partnership with employers leading to a university degree. The programmes are at ISCED levels 5-7, but the overwhelming majority of students are at ISCED levels 6-7. Students spend most of their four-year programmes with their employer, with different release schedules for education at the university. About half of the higher education institutions in Scotland are already involved in the programmes. The programme has grown rapidly, so that in the third year of delivery in 2019/20 there were 1 160 starts on the programme. Graduate apprenticeships are mostly provided in the fields of business management, engineering and IT.
>
> Source: OECD (2020[5]), *Strengthening Skills in Scotland: OECD Review of the Apprenticeship System in Scotland*, https://www.oecd.org/skills/centre-for-skills/Strengthening_Skills_in_Scotland.pdf; Entreprendre (2022[6]), *Contrat d'apprentissage et de professionnalisation : quelles différences ?*, https://entreprendre.service-public.fr/vosdroits/F31704; StudyCHECK.de (2022[7]), *Duales Studium* [Dual study programmes], https://www.studycheck.de/duales-studium.

A third form of work-based learning is the requirement to have relevant professional experience – past work experience, current employment relevant to the targeted programme or both. For example, professional examinations often require several years of work experience, depending on the targeted qualification. In Germany such work experience accounts for about 60% of total programme duration in the case of Master craftsman examinations. As there is no set coursework, the overall programme duration covers the period relevant employment (work-based learning) and preparation for the examination through optional courses. In Switzerland, the required minimum work experience is typically around two years for professional examinations, while programmes in PET colleges are pursued part-time by most participants, who work in a company parallel to their studies (or else they must pursue an internship). Similarly, in Denmark, part-time students in professional bachelor's programmes must have relevant work experience and the programme is delivered so as to build on that work experience (e.g. assignments linked to students' work).

Data on participation in work-based learning could, in principle, provide a valuable guide to the extent of work-based learning, and the different forms it may take, including the length of placements. Such data are not systematically collected for tertiary programmes. Nonetheless, some insights are available from the 2016 ad-hoc module on young people on the labour market of the European Labour Force Survey. It included a few questions about respondents' work experience during their studies (highest completed education). Figure 4.1 shows the share of young people who had work experience during their highest level of tertiary studies. The data distinguish between work-based learning that was connected to the respondent's studies ("work-based learning"), or was not connected to their studies ("outside curriculum", such as having a student job at the cafeteria). Work-based learning in this figure may refer to very short periods – the 25% threshold in Table 4.1 and Table 4.2 does not apply here, but Figure 4.2 provides a more detailed picture, indicating the length of the work-based learning period. This figure refers to all tertiary levels (irrespective of the orientation of the programme) – any work experience that individuals had prior to their highest completed programme is not captured here.

On average over 40% of tertiary graduates report having pursued some form of work-based learning as part of the programme leading to their highest qualification. There is substantial variation across countries, with work-based learning reported by the majority of students in ten countries, while in seven countries a quarter or less of respondents report such experience. On average 29% of respondents in EU Member countries report having pursued work that was not part of their study programme, and a the same share of graduates did not pursue any form of work during their latest studies.

Figure 4.1. Distribution of work experience during tertiary studies (2016)

25-34 year-olds

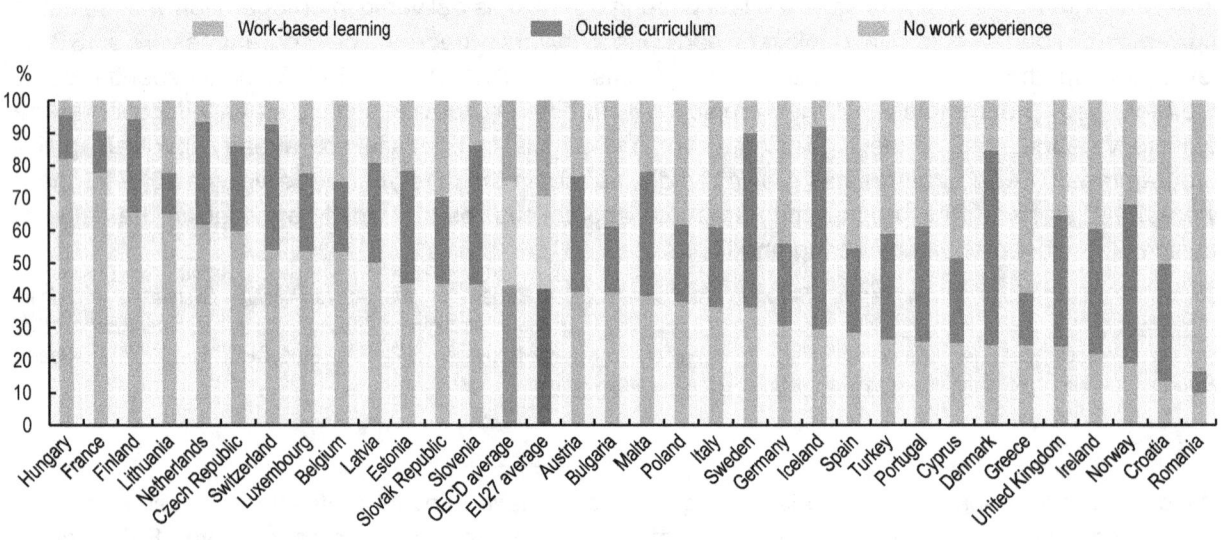

Note: Data for Croatia have limited reliability due to small sample sizes.
Source: European Union Labour Force Survey ad hoc module on young people on the labour market (2016).

StatLink https://stat.link/3dw2tg

Within the "work-based learning" category reported above, data allow to distinguish between types, based on the payment the person received and the duration of work-based learning. Based on these data, a distinction has been drawn by Eurostat (Eurostat, 2016[8]) between the following types of work-based learning:

- Apprenticeships: paid work-based learning with at least 6 months duration that is mandatory part of the curriculum.
- Mandatory traineeships: unpaid work-based learning with at least 6 months duration.
- Optional traineeships: work experience that was an optional part of the curriculum, without further information on duration or pay.
- Other forms of mandatory work-based learning: mandatory part of the curriculum, but with no further information on duration or pay.

As shown in Figure 4.2, mandatory traineeships are most commonly used in tertiary programmes and optional traineeships are also frequent. The definition of "apprenticeship" in these data is relatively broad. It not only includes classical apprenticeship arrangements as set out in Box 4.2, but also longer paid internships – for example a professional bachelor's programme including a 6-month internship would fall in this category.

Figure 4.2. Type of work-based learning experience during tertiary studies (2016)

25-34 year-olds who report work-based learning during tertiary studies

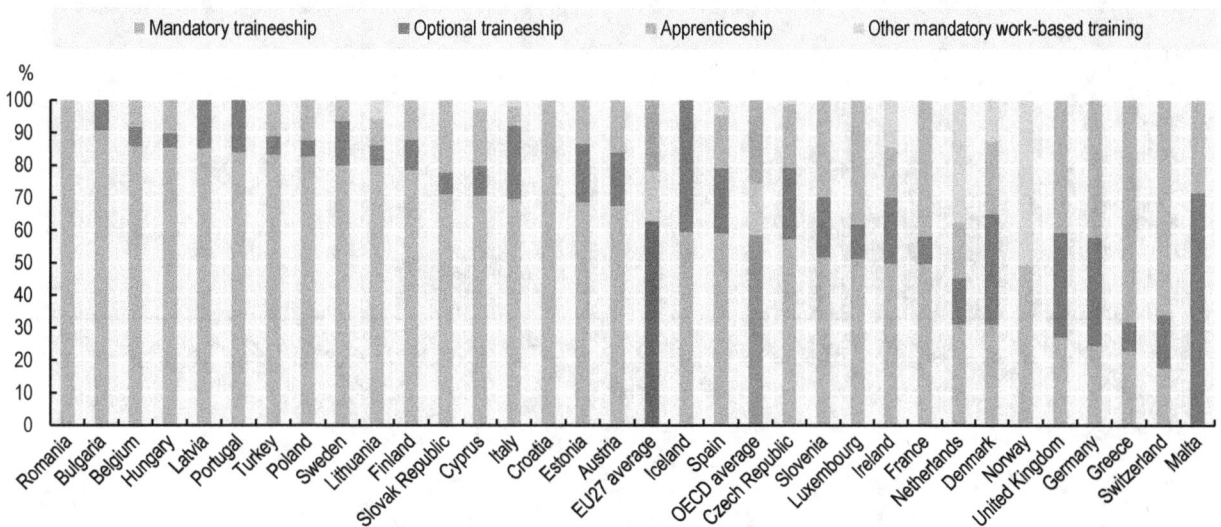

Note: Low reliability due to small sample sizes for the following categories: Mandatory traineeship: Croatia; Optional traineeship: Bulgaria, Luxembourg, Slovenia; Apprenticeship: Croatia, Estonia, Latvia, Malta; Other mandatory work-based training: Cyprus, Czech Republic, Lithuania.
Source: European Union Labour Force Survey ad hoc module on young people on the labour market (2016).

StatLink ⇒ https://stat.link/pdso6f

Targeted fields of study

This section provides insights from comparative data on the different fields of study within professional programmes and explores their relevance to labour market needs. These data are limited to ISCED level 5, which this report treats as professional regardless of how they are classified by the country in comparative data collections. Data on enrolment or graduation by field of study at ISCED level 6 and above cannot be broken down by programme orientation.[1]

Figure 4.3 shows the distribution of graduates in the fields of study with the most graduates at ISCED level 5 and 6. The figure uses data on graduates rather than students, so that the results are not affected by the duration of programmes. Among short-cycle tertiary programmes there is considerable variation in the breadth of the fields covered by programmes. A few countries offer only highly specialised programmes at this level, such as the Czech Republic, where conservatory programmes focus on performing arts and colleges of health and welfare in Poland (Belgium used to provide a narrow range of short-cycle tertiary programmes, but recently introduced a new set of associate degrees in a wider range of fields of study – not yet covered by these data). Compared to upper secondary VET, engineering, manufacturing and construction represents a smaller part of the offer: while 33% of upper secondary VET students graduate from the field of engineering, manufacturing and construction (OECD, 2020[9]), only about 15% of graduates in short-cycle education and in bachelor's programme have studies in this field. The most common field of study at these levels of education is business, administration and law, with about 25% of students on average across OECD countries.

Figure 4.3. Distribution of graduates by field of study at short-cycle tertiary and bachelor's or equivalent level (2018)

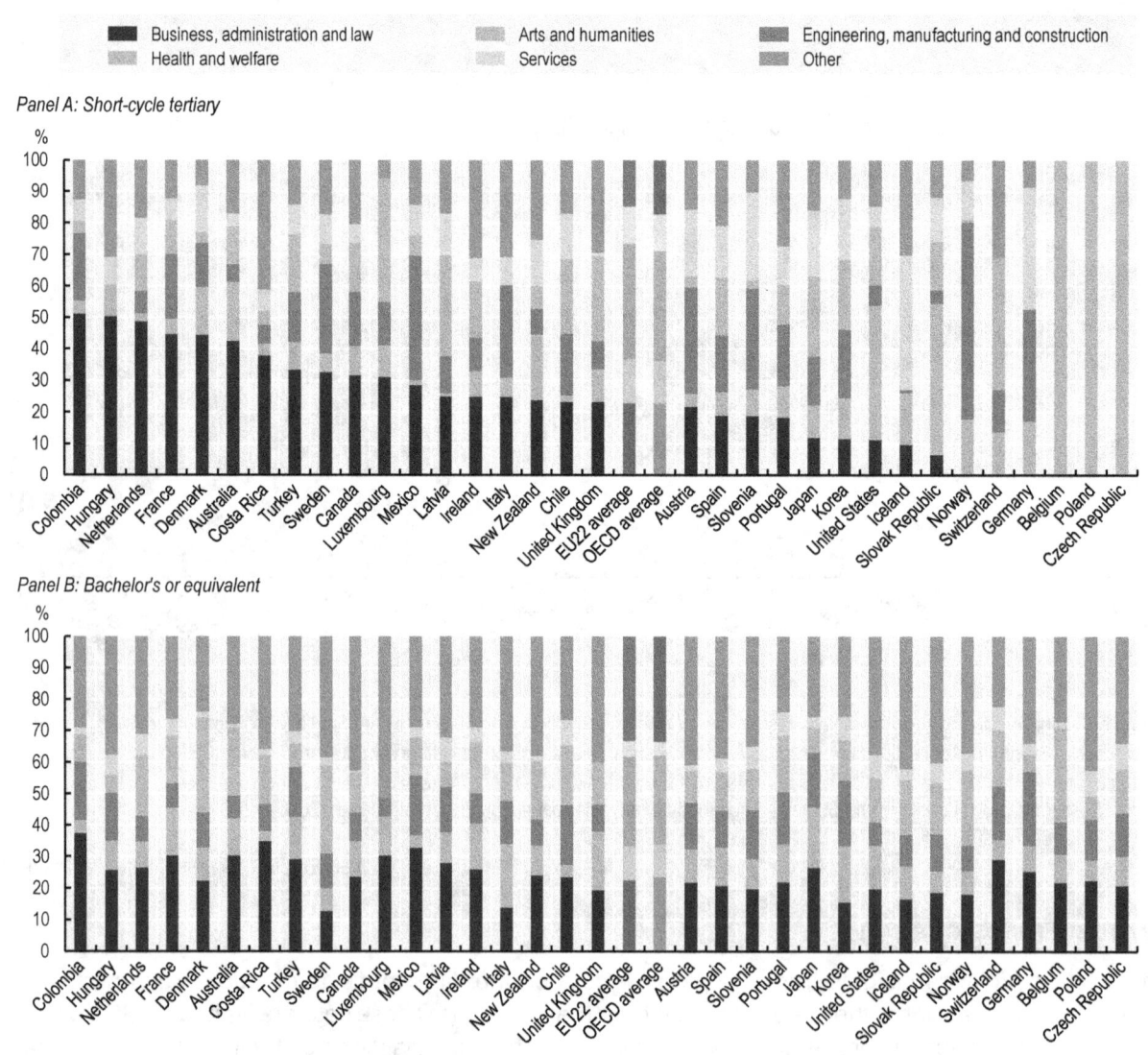

Source: OECD (2020[10]) Education at a Glance", Education and Training – Education at a Glance (database), https://stats.oecd.org/.

StatLink https://stat.link/16y8hr

Figure 4.4 explores to what extent students enter fields of study with the most attractive labour market prospects – the data focus on earnings, recognising that the attractiveness of different career options also depends on many other factors. It focuses on entrants (rather than students or graduates) to capture student choices, rather than the output of the system. The figure shows the relationship between the share of entrants to different fields of study at short-cycle tertiary level and earnings of graduates in those fields. Students' choices of field of study are clearly not solely driven by economic considerations. For example, on average across the 11 OECD countries with data on earnings by field of study, about the same share of students enter short-cycle tertiary programmes in the field of education as in the field of ICT despite the much larger financial returns in the ICT field.

Figure 4.4. Relationship between the share of short-cycle tertiary new entrants and relative earnings, by field of study (2017)

Average by field among countries with available data

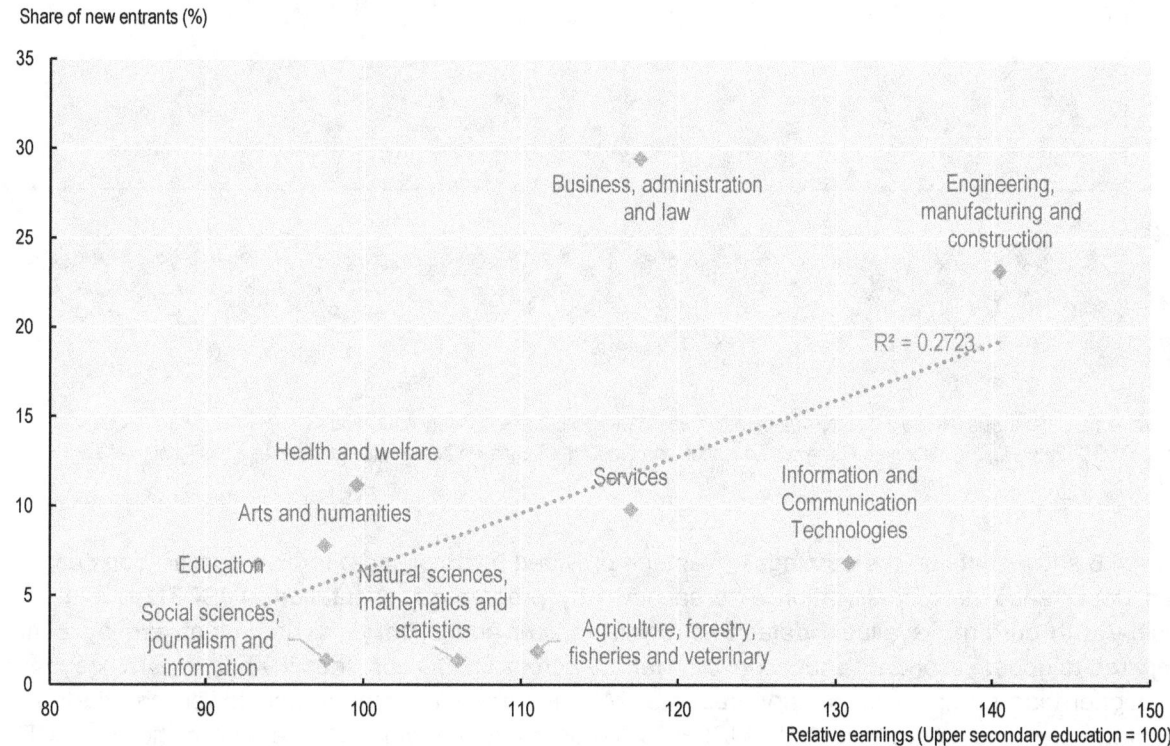

Note: Averages are based on data from Australia, Austria, Chile, Costa Rica, Denmark, Estonia, Finland, Latvia, Norway, Sweden and the United Kingdom.
Source: OECD (2020[10]), "Education at a Glance", Education and Training – Education at a Glance (database), https://stats.oecd.org/.

StatLink https://stat.link/xpg03n

Outcomes from professional tertiary education

This section explores data on outcomes from professional tertiary education, focusing mostly on employment outcomes. The figures only identify short-cycle tertiary programmes as professional – ISCED 5 programmes when the analysis is based on the ISCED 2011 framework, and ISCED 5B programmes when the analysis is based on the earlier ISCED 97 framework (the two categories are not perfect equivalents but are similar). Within ISCED 6 programmes, it was not possible to identify data for professional programmes.

In nearly all OECD countries, adults with short-cycle tertiary qualifications have higher employment rates than those holding only an upper secondary qualification (Figure 4.5). For EU countries on average the benefit, in terms of higher employment, is almost as high as for ISCED level 6 qualifications, although there is substantial variation across countries. Data are collected by orientation at ISCED level 6, but are not presented here, because meaningful comparisons are very difficult.[2]

Figure 4.5. Employment rate of tertiary-educated adults relative to adults with upper secondary education (2019)

25-64 year-olds; upper secondary education = 100

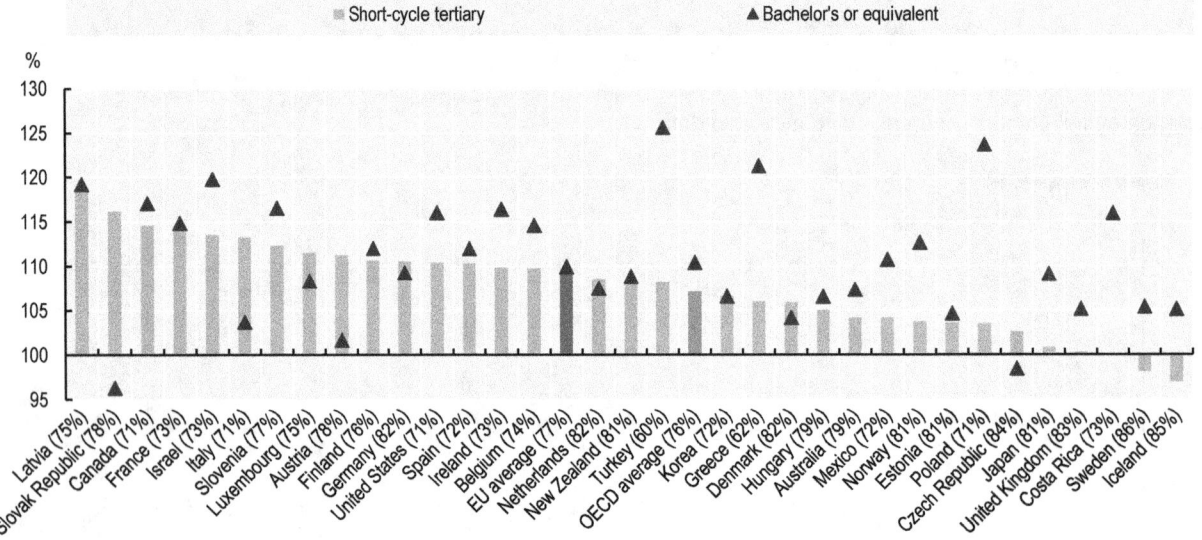

Note: Values in parenthesis refer to the employment rate of adults with an upper secondary education.
Source: OECD (2020[10]), "Education at a Glance", Education and Training – Education at a Glance (database), https://stats.oecd.org/.

StatLink https://stat.link/ebf4t2

Figure 4.6 shows data on the earnings advantage provided by obtaining a tertiary qualification compared to an upper secondary qualification. A breakdown by programme orientation at ISCED level 6 is not possible with currently available data. Short-cycle tertiary education yields important earning benefits compared to upper secondary education: on average across OECD countries it leads to earnings that are 19% higher than for upper secondary graduates. At the same time, they remain lower than the earning advantage provided by qualifications at ISCED level 6 and above (earnings are 43% higher for ISCED 6 graduates and 89% higher for graduates of ISCED 7 and above than for upper secondary graduates). These averages hide differences between fields of study. As shown in Figure 4.4, earnings differ substantially between fields of study at the short-cycle tertiary level.

Students who had work experience during their studies tend to have higher employment rates than those who did not (see Figure 4.7). Those who pursued apprenticeship-type programmes[3] have the highest employment rates. Mandatory traineeships are also associated with better outcomes than programmes without work experience. Pursuing work even outside the curriculum is also linked to better outcomes than not having any work experience while studying, possibly because such experience may develop more general employability skills, such as teamwork[4]. Some national studies also looked at the outcomes associated with the use of work-based learning. For example, a recent study of 2 and 3-year professional tertiary programmes in France (Couppié and Gasquet, 2021[11]) found that graduates who pursued a dual pathway were more likely to be employed in a job relevant to their qualification and were more often employed by the company where they pursued their training than those who pursued the mainly university-based option (with an internship).

Figure 4.6. Earnings of tertiary-educated adults relative to adults with upper secondary education (2018)

25-64 year-old full-time and full-year workers; upper secondary education = 100

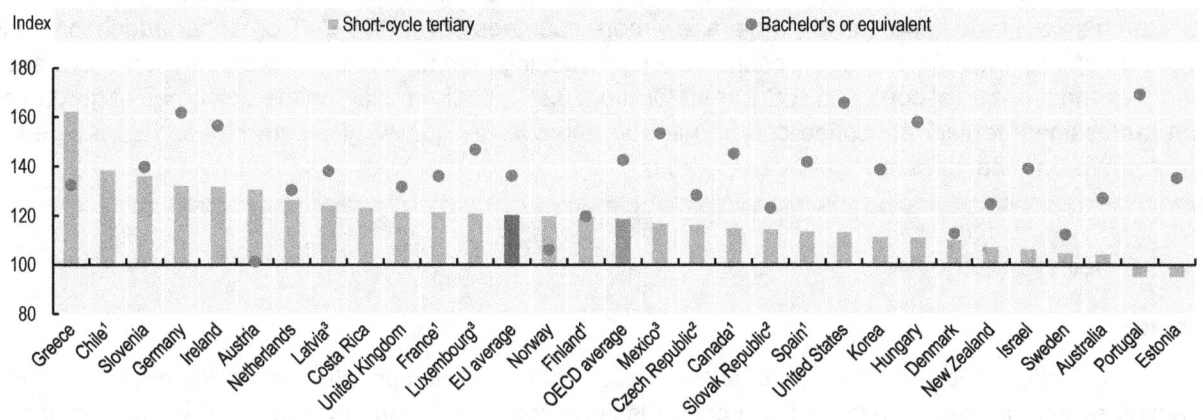

Note: The following data point are not displayed on the chart because they are above 180: Chile (279 - Bachelor's or equivalent), Costa Rica (199 – Bachelor's or equivalent).
1. Year of reference differs from 2018.
2. Index 100 refers to the combined ISCED levels 3 and 4 of the educational attainment levels in the ISCED 2011 classification.
3. Earnings net of income tax.
Source: OECD (2020[10]), "Education at a Glance", Education and Training – Education at a Glance (database), https://stats.oecd.org/.

StatLink https://stat.link/47cf2n

Figure 4.7. Employment rate by work experience during tertiary studies (2016)

25-34 year-olds

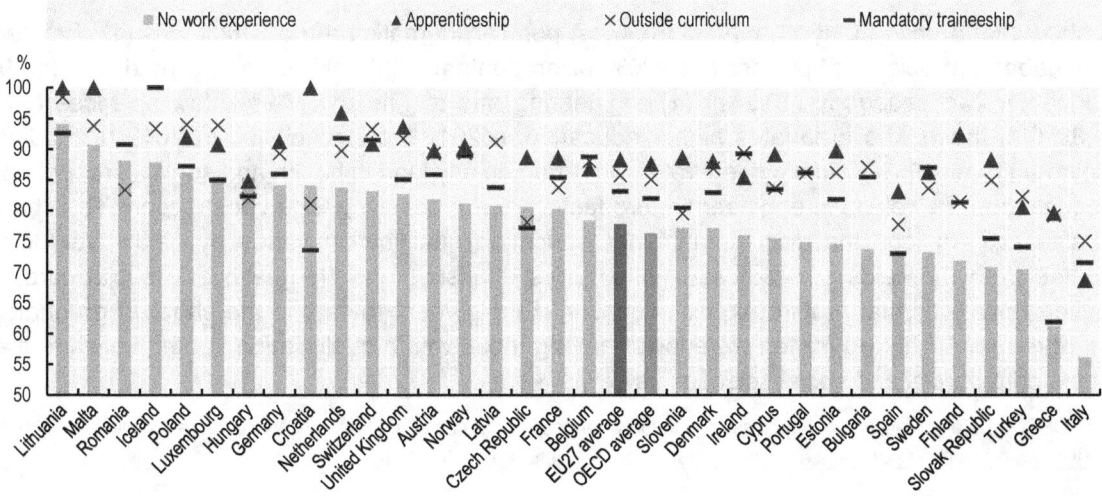

Note: Low reliability due to small sample sizes for the following categories: Apprenticeship: Croatia, Estonia, Malta; Mandatory traineeship: Croatia.
Source: European Union Labour Force Survey ad hoc module on young people on the labour market (2016).

StatLink https://stat.link/kxhlw1

To monitor the outcomes of students, a number of countries have graduate tracking systems in place, focusing on VET, higher education or both. There are also major ongoing efforts to further develop such systems in a way that will allow for the collection of comparative indicators at the European level. According to the recently published paper by an international expert group dedicated to support these efforts (EC Expert Group, 2021[12]), a two-step approach is desirable: in the short-term countries should use a European survey of graduates, and in the medium-term countries should adapt administrative data so that they can underpin comparative indicators. Currently 18 member states and European Economic Area countries have graduate tracking systems in place covering VET and higher education (Box 4.3 describes the examples of France and Latvia), while a few more countries cover only VET or higher education. This is an area of ongoing reform in many countries – new tracking measures are in development or have been announced in a dozen of countries (EC Expert Group, 2021[12]). Information on the outcomes of graduates from professional tertiary education can be used to improve the quality of programmes, the change the mix of provision, and for career guidance purposes.

Box 4.3. Graduate tracking

France

Since the early 1990s, a survey (*Enquête Génération*) targets young people who left the education and training system in the same year. Each cohort is surveyed 3, 5, 7 and sometimes 10 years after they left the education and training system. The survey is designed to explore transition to employment and inform the evaluation and development of employment and training policy. The data collection concerns education and training pathways, work activities, personal and household characteristics. Additional modules explore specific themes.

Latvia

Graduate tracking was introduced in 2018. The ministry provides the data about graduates to the National Statistical Bureau, which connects this data with the data on income from the State Revenue Service, data on employment status from the National Employment Agency and data from other state registers. The data are analysed at individual level and published in an aggregated, anonymous way. This allows each higher education institution to observe the employment rate and average income of their graduates, as well as whether they work in a job that requires higher education.

Data show that among 2018 graduates, the most popular thematic area of study was (1) commercial and management sciences/ professions (20% of graduates); (2) health care and medicine (14.9%); (3) education and pedagogy (10.2%); (4) engineering and technology (7.9%); law sciences (7.3%). Over 80% of those who graduates higher education in 2018 were employed in 2019 (the adjusted employment rate is 88%). Employment rates were particularly high in health and social care, education and agriculture, as well as in engineering, production and processing, and construction. The share of graduates holding jobs that require a higher education qualification varies by field: over 80% of graduates from the fields of sciences, mathematics, statistics and IT, health and social care, and education have jobs that require higher education. Employment rates and the share of graduates in jobs that require higher education were lower among those with a qualification in humanities and arts; services; commercial and social sciences, law.

Source: OECD Data collection on professional tertiary education; Céreq (2022[13]), *Insertion professionnelle (Génération)*, https://www.cereq.fr/enquetes-et-donnees/insertion-professionnelle-generation.

Based on national data, some further insights are available on outcomes from different types of tertiary education. Box 4.4 provides some examples – recognising that Finland currently reports UAS programmes under "unspecified orientation".

> **Box 4.4. National evidence on outcomes from applied or professional tertiary education**
>
> **Finland**
>
> Universities of applied sciences (or (or polytechnics) were established in 1991 to offer bachelor's degrees, which take 3.5-4 years to complete. A study based on longitudinal register data (Böckerman, Haapanen and Jepsen, 2018[14]) found it led to significant gains in employment outcomes compared to adults with similar pre-enrolment characteristics who did not pursue studies after upper secondary education. For younger persons (aged 19-24 at entry), it found an increase in annual earnings of EUR 1 300 five years after entry and EUR 3 300 ten years after entry, as well as higher employment rates (by 5.1 and 6.6 percentage points respectively). For older students (aged 25-50 at entry), the increase in annual earnings was almost EUR 2 700 five years after entry and over EUR 3 700 ten years after entry. The benefits in terms of employment rates were modest (1.5 to 2.5 percentage points respectively).
>
> Vocational master's programmes were first piloted in 2002 and rolled out, enrolling 4 300 students in 2016. They are provided in universities of applied sciences, which also provide vocational bachelor's qualifications. Entry requires a vocational bachelor's degree and three years of work experience. A study (Böckerman, Haapanen and Jepsen, 2019[15]) explored the associated labour market outcomes analysing longitudinal register data. It found that obtaining a vocational master's qualification led to a 7% earnings increase four to six years after entry. Attendees received higher earnings regardless of whether they switch employers, and the gains were similar by gender and age. Vocational master's degrees also appeared to help individuals advance in their careers: they were more likely to move up the occupational hierarchy (e.g. to become managers) than those with similar pre-enrolment characteristics who did not pursue a vocational master's qualification.
>
> **France**
>
> Graduates of professional bachelor's programmes commonly pursue further studies: 41% started a new programme within 30 months of graduation. Among those who entered the labour market, 92% were employed, with the highest employment rates among science, technology and healthcare graduates and those in the fields of law, economics and management. Graduates in the fields of humanities and social sciences had lower employment rates. The majority find that their employment matches their level of qualification (77%) and is relevant to their field of study (82%). Nearly 90% of graduates work in the private sector.
>
> Source: Böckerman, Haapanen and Jepsen (2018[14]), *More skilled, better paid: labour-market returns to postsecondary vocational education*, https://ideas.repec.org/s/oup/oxecpp.html; Böckerman, Haapanen and Jepsen (2019[15]), *Back to school: Labor-market returns to higher vocational schooling*, https://doi.org/10.1016/j.labeco.2019.101758; SIES (2021[16]), *Légère baisse de l'insertion des diplômés de licence professionnelle au 1er décembre 2020*, https://www.enseignementsup-recherche.gouv.fr/sites/default/files/2021-12/nf-sies-2021-28-15586.pdf.

Wages are not the only element to consider when analysing the quality of employment. The OECD job quality framework includes, alongside the obvious dimension of earnings, labour market security and the quality of the working environment. On various potential measures of job quality (e.g. job satisfaction, open-ended contracts) data are available from the Survey of Adult Skills, a product of the Programme for the International Assessment of Adult Competencies (PIAAC). Our analysis found few differences between graduates of different levels of tertiary education – but this may just reflect that the categories of education background (i.e. ISCED-97 5A and 5B) were not suited to capture variation in this regard. Therefore, only one measure of job quality is presented here, in addition to the earnings data presented above, to give a flavour of the data available in this area. Figure 4.8 shows a measure of work strain: the share of those working over 50 hours per week. Variation is larger between countries than within countries by educational background. However, in several countries (e.g. France, Korea, Turkey, United States) short-cycle graduates more often have longer working hours than graduates of ISCED level 6 programmes. In some countries, there is little difference by tertiary level or the relationship is reversed with bachelor's level graduates more commonly working over 50 hours per week (e.g. Denmark, Ireland, Japan).

Figure 4.8. Share of workers working more than 50 hours per week, by tertiary educational attainment (2012, 2015 or 2017)

16-65 year-old non-students

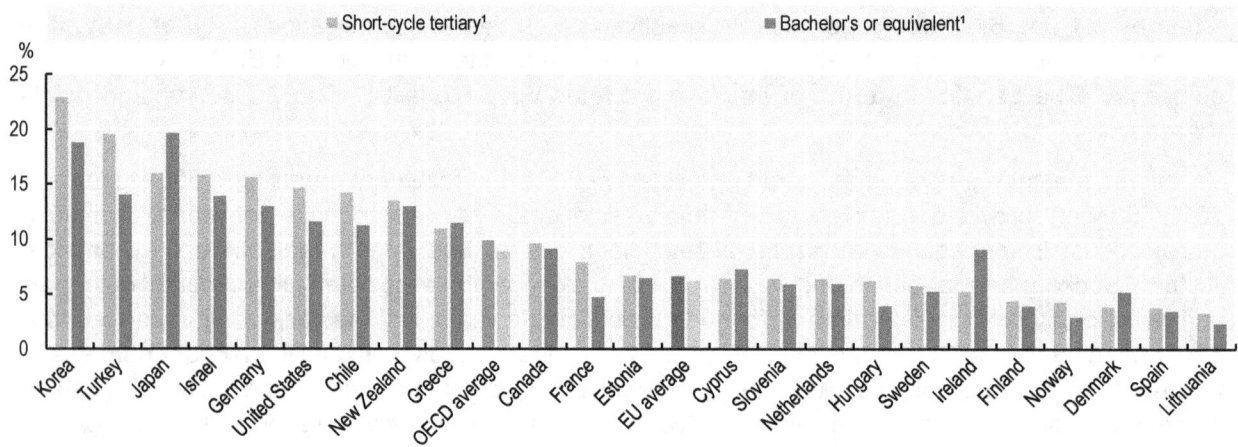

Note: Data refer to 2015 for Chile, Greece, Israel, Lithuania, New Zealand, Slovenia and Turkey. Data refer to 2017 for Hungary and the United States. All other countries refer to 2012. The number of working hours per week was capped at 80. The Survey of Adult Skills (PIAAC) is based on ISCED-97 and uses pre-Bologna classification of tertiary education. The labels have been adapted in this chart, so that they use the closest equivalents: short-cycle tertiary education = ISCED-97 5B, Bachelor's or equivalent = ISCED-97 5A.
Source: OECD Survey of Adult Skills (PIAAC), https://www.oecd.org/skills/piaac/.

StatLink https://stat.link/w3i6f4

To measure the quality of professional programmes, one could also look at the skills of their graduates. However, data on the skills of graduates are very limited. At an international level, direct measures of graduate skills are only available regarding generic skills: the Survey of Adult Skills (PIAAC) provides insights on literacy, numeracy and problem-solving by educational background. The main potential strength of professional programmes is their capacity to develop specific skills that will enable graduates to smoothly transition to employment in a profession or a specific sector. Such skills are not directly measured by currently available data, and for understandable reasons – establishing the specific skills needed by tertiary graduates and developing reliable comparative measures would be extremely hard.

At the same time, all adults, including those with professional qualifications, need sound basic skills to function as members of society and pursue successful career. Figure 4.9 shows the mean literacy scores of tertiary education graduates, showing substantial variation across countries and revealing relatively low mean scores among short-cycle tertiary graduates in particular. These results do not simply capture the skills-developing impact of different types of tertiary education. They also reflect selection and self-selection into different pathways: upper secondary graduates with stronger literacy and numeracy skills are more likely to enter higher levels of education, while tertiary students with weak basic skills are more likely to drop out. As indicated earlier by Figure 2.13, in some countries a considerable share of upper secondary graduates (and VET graduates in particular) leave the school system with weak basic skills. Professional tertiary education programmes are often viewed as a vehicle for social mobility and inclusiveness. To exploit their full potential in this role, professional programmes need to identify weaknesses in the basic skills of entrants and offer students support to help fill skills gaps. Differences in skill levels in Figure 4.9 may not only reflect differences in the extent to which these skills were developed in the education system, but also the extent to which individuals continued to develop or maintain their skills during working life.

Figure 4.9. Mean literacy score by level of educational attainment (2012, 2015 or 2017)

Adults aged 16-65

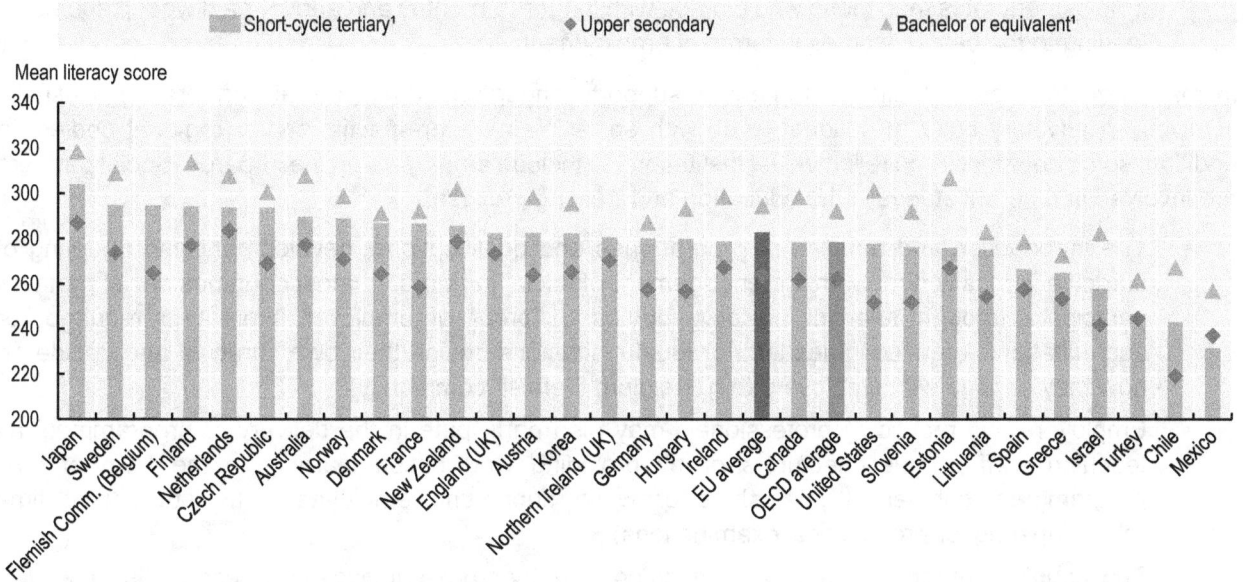

Note: Data refer to 2015 for Chile, Greece, Israel, Lithuania, New Zealand, Slovenia and Turkey. Data refer to 2017 for Hungary, Mexico, and the United States. All other countries refer to 2012.
1. The Survey of Adult Skills (PIAAC) is based on ISCED-97 and uses pre-Bologna classification of tertiary education. The labels have been adapted in this chart, so that they use the closest equivalents: short-cycle tertiary education = ISCED-97 5B, Bachelor's or equivalent = ISCED-97 5A.
Source: OECD Survey of Adult Skills (PIAAC), https://www.oecd.org/skills/piaac/.

StatLink https://stat.link/m95cq3

Conclusion

Work-based learning (in real workplaces rather than simulated work environments) is a powerful tool for connecting professional programmes to the world of work:

- Work-based learning is commonly an element in professional tertiary programmes, but is not always mandatory. For example, associate degrees in several countries require a mandatory internship that accounts for a quarter or a third of programme duration. However, in some countries the use of work-based learning remains patchy.
- At ISCED level 6 work-based learning is less common than at level 5. Professional bachelor's programmes include mandatory internships in several countries, or may be pursued through a dual

pathway (e.g. professional bachelor's degrees in France may pursued through either of those options). In many countries, the use of work-based learning is not systematic, only used in specific fields or remains optional.

- Dual tertiary programmes have been growing across OECD countries, with several countries providing dual options at ISCED level 6 (and a few even at ISCED level 7), though such programmes are often reported as having "academic" or "unspecified" orientation.

- When students pursue professional programmes with relevant work experience (as regular employees rather than as apprentices or trainees), their employment is often acknowledged as a form of work-based learning. In several countries, students with past or ongoing employment receive exemptions from mandatory internships. In professional examinations, having relevant work experience is the only possible route to the qualification.

- Adults who benefited from work-based learning during their tertiary studies tend to have higher employment rates than those who did not, with longer (6 months and above) paid work placements leading to the best outcomes in terms of employment.

In many countries an institutional framework supports engagement with social partners. This usually involves an advisory body at national level, with sometimes sector-specific and/or regional bodies. In addition, some countries require individual institutions to include employers on their boards. Social partners are involved in different stages in the education and training process:

- The introduction and removal of programmes and qualifications, development and updating of curricula is mostly done with the engagement of social partners. In most countries social partners participate through relevant advisory bodies or proof of employer interest is required for accreditation. A few countries let individual institutions design their own curricula and decide on how they engage with employers (e.g. Belgium Flemish community).

- Employers and practicing professionals may also participate in the delivery of programmes: as teaching staff or guest lecturers or by providing work-based learning in the form of dual programmes, substantial internships or while supporting employees who study part time (e.g. preparing for professional examinations).

- Few countries report systematically engaging industry representatives in assessments. However, in the case of professional examinations, industry representatives are strongly engaged in the development of the assessment framework as well as conducting assessments as examiners.

Data on outcomes from professional tertiary education are available only for short-cycle tertiary programmes (a breakdown by orientation is available for employment rates at ISCED level 6 but not included here due to data quality issues).

- Graduates of short-cycle tertiary education have higher employment rates than those holding an upper secondary qualification, and on average across EU member states their employment rate is nearly as high as those of ISCED level 6 graduates (and in a few countries it is higher). In terms of earnings graduates of bachelor's level programmes do better than short-cycle tertiary graduates, with the exception of a small number of countries, but earn less than ISCED level 6 graduates.

- The earnings advantage provided by short-cycle tertiary studies relative to an upper secondary qualification varies considerably across different fields of study. It is highest in the field of engineering, manufacturing and construction, and in ICT. Fields like education, social sciences, journalism and information and arts and humanities yield the lowest earnings advantages.

References

Böckerman, P., M. Haapanen and C. Jepsen (2019), "Back to school: Labor-market returns to higher vocational schooling", *Labour Economics*, Vol. 61, https://doi.org/10.1016/j.labeco.2019.101758. [15]

Böckerman, P., M. Haapanen and C. Jepsen (2018), "More skilled, better paid: labour-market returns to postsecondary vocational education", *Oxford Economic Papers*, Vol. 70/2, pp. 485-508, https://ideas.repec.org/s/oup/oxecpp.html. [14]

Céreq (2022), *Insertion professionnelle (Génération)*, https://www.cereq.fr/enquetes-et-donnees/insertion-professionnelle-generation (accessed on 15 February 2022). [13]

Couppié, T. and C. Gasquet (2021), "Débuter en CDI : le plus des apprentis", *Bulletin de Recherches Emploi Formation*, No. 406, Céreq, https://www.cereq.fr/debuter-en-cdi-le-plus-des-apprentis#.YlWXsZGtWvI.link. [11]

EC Expert Group (2021), *Towards a European graduate tracking mechanism - Publications Office of the EU*, Publications Office of the European Union, Luxembourg, https://doi.org/10.2766/970793. [12]

Entreprendre (2022), *Contrat d'apprentissage et de professionnalisation : quelles différences ?*, https://entreprendre.service-public.fr/vosdroits/F31704 (accessed on 15 February 2022). [6]

Eurostat (2016), *Eurostat metadata. 2016 Young people on the labour market (lfso_16)*, https://ec.europa.eu/eurostat/cache/metadata/en/lfso_16_esms.htm. [8]

Muehlemann, S. and M. Leiser (2015), "Ten Facts You Need To Know About Hiring", http://ftp.iza.org/dp9363.pdf (accessed on 25 January 2018). [2]

OECD (2021), *OECD Data collection on professional tertiary education*, Unpublished. [17]

OECD (2020), *"Education at a Glance", Education and Training – Education at a Glance (database)*, https://stats.oecd.org/ (accessed on 1 June 2021). [10]

OECD (2020), *Education at a Glance 2020: OECD Indicators*, OECD Publishing, Paris, https://doi.org/10.1787/69096873-en. [9]

OECD (2020), *Strengthening Skills in Scotland: OECD Review of the Apprenticeship System in Scotland*, OECD, Paris, https://www.oecd.org/skills/centre-for-skills/Strengthening_Skills_in_Scotland.pdf. [5]

OECD (2017), *OECD Handbook for Internationally Comparative Education Statistics: Concepts, Standards, Definitions and Classifications*, OECD Publishing, Paris, https://doi.org/10.1787/9789264279889-en. [4]

OECD (2014), *Skills Beyond School: Synthesis Report*, OECD Publishing, Paris, http://http//dx.doi.org/10.1787/9789264214682-en. [3]

SIES (2021), "Légère baisse de l'insertion des diplômés de licence professionnelle au 1er décembre 2020", *Note Flash du SIES*, No. 28, Ministère de l'Enseignement Supérieur, de la Recherche et de l'Innovation, https://www.enseignementsup-recherche.gouv.fr/sites/default/files/2021-12/nf-sies-2021-28-15586.pdf (accessed on 17 December 2021). [16]

StudyCHECK.de (2022), *Duales Studium*, https://www.studycheck.de/duales-studium (accessed on 15 February 2022). [7]

Ulicna, D., K. Luomi Messerer and M. Auzinger (2016), *Study on higher Vocational Education and Training in the EU*, European Commission, Brussels, https://doi.org/10.2767/421741. [1]

Notes

[1] Although the ISCED-F 2013 could be used, in theory, to help identify programmes with professional orientation, most countries report data based on highly aggregated 1-digit categories based on the ISCED-F2013 framework. Some of the categories are mostly sector- or profession-oriented (e.g. "Engineering, manufacturing and construction", "Health and welfare"), but others contain a mix.

[2] Not only internationally agreed definitions are lacking but in some countries the data reported are inconsistent with classification choices in ISCED mappings.

[3] Based on the operational definition by Eurostat: paid work-based learning with at least 6 months duration that is mandatory part of the curriculum.

[4] There is some ambiguity regarding the categorisation of employment that is relevant to tertiary studies and is pursued in parallel – examples would include adults who work while pursuing preparatory courses for professional examinations (e.g. Germany, Switzerland) or adults who work in an occupation relevant to their programme and study part-time (e.g. part-time professional bachelor's programmes in Denmark). However, for both professional examinations and part-time programmes combined with relevant employment, work experience is an entry requirement rather than part of the curriculum in a strict sense. It is therefore unclear whether such cases are systematically reported under one category, and if so, whether that category is "apprenticeship" or work-based learning "outside curriculum".

5 Key findings and proposals for the classification of tertiary programmes by orientation

This chapter presents key findings from comparative data on professional tertiary education and advances proposals for the development of internationally agreed definitions for programme orientation at tertiary levels. Countries report a wide range of programmes as professional, including one- or two-year programmes, professional bachelor's degrees and professional examinations, which upskill existing professionals. Comparative data provide some insights into the functions of professional programmes, the profile of learners, pathways leading into programmes and associated outcomes. However, huge gaps remain in data because of the lack of internationally agreed definitions for programme orientation at tertiary levels. This report proposes a three-way classification of programmes, to distinguish between profession-oriented (e.g. training for nurses and interior designers), sector-oriented (e.g. food technology, business studies) and general (e.g. history, physics) programmes.

This report surveyed the field of professional tertiary education. This field emerged as the result of the diversification of tertiary education systems in particular throughout the 20th century. As tertiary programmes became increasingly connected to employment opportunities, many countries introduced shorter programmes, which in one or two years prepared individuals for working in particular occupations. Across countries these include associate degrees in Belgium and the Netherlands, higher vocational education and training (VET) programmes in Austria, Norway, Slovenia and Sweden.

At bachelor's level, the landscape includes professional bachelor's degrees, which are often taught in a separate tier of institutions, such as universities of applied sciences or university colleges. These institutions focus on applied, practically-oriented teaching and conducting less research than regular universities. But in countries with unified tertiary education systems, like the United States, the kinds of applied programmes taught at these institutions are more often delivered in regular universities, which provide a wide range of programmes, from occupationally-focused bachelor's programmes to PhD qualifications.

In addition, professional examinations represent a distinct family of qualifications. Unlike the programmes described above, they have few or no required coursework requirements, although participants usually pursue preparatory courses and several years of relevant work experience is an entry requirement. Such examinations (e.g. master craftsman qualifications in Germany, federal examinations in Switzerland) are a key path to advanced technical and managerial skills for graduates of upper secondary VET, not just in "traditional" vocational fields but also in emerging fields like finance.

This diverse landscape, the students it serves and the outcomes it leads to remains poorly measured by comparative data. The introduction of the ISCED 2011 framework created an opportunity to collect better data on professional tertiary education, by allowing for different programme orientations at all levels. This report has explored data provided by countries on professional programmes: it included all short-cycle tertiary programmes (as this level is predominantly professional) and ISCED level 6 programmes that countries have chosen to classify as professional.

Key conclusions from the data analysis include:

- Professional programmes play a key role in upskilling VET graduates. They are sometimes the only type of tertiary education directly accessible from VET, and in some cases they provide a bridge into the academic sector of higher education, thus facilitating permeability.
- Having past or current work experience is common among tertiary students, especially among those with a vocational upper secondary background, who are also more likely to have held high-skilled jobs than those with a general education background.
- Younger adults dominate in programmes providing initial preparation for labour market entry, both short-cycle tertiary programmes and professional bachelor's programmes in various European countries. Older adults dominate in programmes offering other functions, including upskilling for existing professionals (e.g. professional examinations) and reskilling for adults.
- Work-based learning is commonly an element in professional tertiary programmes especially at ISCED level 5, but is not always mandatory. At ISCED level 6 professional bachelor's programmes often include mandatory internships and dual tertiary programmes have also been growing (though countries do not always classify these as "professional"). Relevant past or current work experience is often acknowledged as a form of work-based learning. In many countries, however, work-based learning is only used in some fields or is optional. Adults who benefited from work-based learning during their tertiary studies tend to have higher employment rates than those who did not, with longer (6 months and above) paid work placements leading to the best outcomes in terms of employment.

However, huge gaps remain because there are no internationally agreed definitions for programme orientation at tertiary level. With currently available data, it is not even possible to establish in a reliable, comparative manner what share of students at bachelor's level pursue programmes with different types of orientation. Programmes preparing for the same professions like teachers, nurses or accountants are classified differently by countries. As a result, for ISCED level 5, data are collected based on the agreed definition of "vocational". But for ISCED level 6 and above, the few countries that provide data do so based on their own national definitions of "professional" and "academic", and some countries prefer not to provide data that could be ambiguous in the absence of agreed definitions.

To address this issue, this report has made proposals for the development of internationally agreed definitions. These proposals are based on consultation with countries[1] to provide an understanding of how programmes with different orientations are provided across countries, and the practical constraints they face for data collections.

The proposal advanced here is to establish a classification based on the professional dimension of programmes for two reasons. First, the academic-professional dichotomy is problematic, because some programmes are both academic (in the sense of highly demanding intellectually) and professional (in that they prepare for a particular profession). Second, operationalising the intellectual complexity of different programmes within each ISCED level would be extraordinarily hard and of questionable value.

The proposal here is to establish a three-way classification. The terminology used for each category is to be agreed in consultation with countries to take into account the different nuances and resonances of particular terms in different languages. One option might be to refer to the categories below as "profession-oriented", "sector-oriented" and "general":

- Type 1: Programmes that provide applied education and training designed to equip students with knowledge and skills required to practice a particular profession.
- Type 2: Programmes that provide applied education and training designed to equip students with knowledge and skills required to work within an occupational family or industrial sector.
- Type 3: Programmes that provide discipline-oriented education in the pure sciences, humanities and arts. While such programmes should also provide knowledge and skills of labour market relevance, these are applicable in very diverse contexts and are not intended to prepare students for a particular profession, occupational family or industrial sector.

Additional indicators could complete this classification, to capture variation in the delivery of programmes and their quality. Examples of such indicators are the share of practical training (in real or simulated work environments, the share of work-based learning (in real workplaces) or the engagement of employers.

In addition, agreeing on the classification of detailed fields of study set out in the ISCED-F framework could help to ensure clarity regarding some numerically large programmes (e.g. teaching, nursing) and facilitate reporting in countries that lack the institutional or programmatic distinctions that could underpin classification.

In practice, classification might be more or less straightforward depending on the design features of programmes and institutional context in different countries. The proposed approach is a pragmatic way to improve the quality and availability of data on professional tertiary education. Various data collections (e.g. UOE, LSO) are already in place and invite countries to provide a breakdown by programme orientation at different tertiary levels. The implementation of these proposals would yield large returns, unlocking the potential of ongoing data collections regarding professional tertiary education.

As tertiary education expands and diversifies, an important question for policy makers is what type of tertiary education can help deliver the desired mix of skills for our economies and societies, balancing the need to ensure smooth entry into employment and prepare for a career shaped by rapid changes in skills needs. While there is spectrum of programmes with different relative degrees of professional orientation, and all programmes aim to lead into employment, there is a major difference between programmes that take their point of departure in an academic discipline (like physics) and those (like teacher education) that are designed around a target occupation (or a small set of target occupations). Better comparative data would help countries measure changes over time in the use of different types of tertiary education, benchmark themselves against other countries, and explore links between different types of tertiary education and various outcomes, such as access to tertiary education or labour market and social outcomes.

Note

[1] Relevant teams within the OECD Directorate for Education and Skills were also consulted, in addition to country consultation through the Ad-hoc Working Group on Professional Tertiary Education.

Annex A. Background information on country inputs

Table A A.1. Countries' input into the project "Higher VET – Professional tertiary education"

	Completed the questionnaire on professional tertiary education	Joined the Ad hoc Working Group on Professional Tertiary Education
OECD		
Australia	x	
Austria	x	x
Belgium	x	x
Canada	x	x
Chile	x	
Colombia	x	x
Costa Rica	x	
Czech Republic	x	
Denmark	x	x
Estonia	x	x
Finland	x	x
France	x	x
Germany	x	x
Greece		
Hungary	x	
Iceland		
Ireland		
Israel	x	x
Italy	x	x
Japan	x	
Korea	x	
Latvia	x	x
Lithuania	x	x
Luxembourg	x	
Mexico	x	
Netherlands	x	
New Zealand	x	x
Norway	x	x
Poland	x	x
Portugal	x	
Slovak Republic	x	
Slovenia	x	x
Spain	x	
Sweden	x	x
Switzerland	x	x
Turkey	x	x
United Kingdom	x	x
United States		x

	Completed the questionnaire on professional tertiary education	Joined the Ad hoc Working Group on Professional Tertiary Education
Partners		
Brazil	x	x
Non-OECD EU member states or candidate countries		
Albania	x	x
Bulgaria		x
Croatia		
Cyprus	x	x
Liechtenstein		
Macedonia		
Malta		
Montenegro		x
Romania		
Serbia		
International organisations		
European Commission		x
European Training Foundation		x
Eurostat		x
TUAC		x
UNESCO		x

Note: Within the OECD, colleagues from the Directorate for Education and Skills also joined meetings of the Ad-hoc Working Group on Professional Tertiary Education.
Source: OECD Data collection on professional tertiary education.

Table A A.2. Academic or professional? Current classification for selected occupations

Orientation attributed to programmes leading to selected occupations in international data collections

	Early childhood teacher	Primary school teacher	Nurse	Medical doctor	Engineer	Lawyer	Accountant
OECD							
Australia	Unspecified	Unspecified	Unspecified	Unspecified	Unspecified	Unspecified	Unspecified
Austria	Professional	Academic	Academic	Academic	Both	Academic	Both
Belgium (French comm.)	Professional	Professional	Professional	Academic	Academic	m	Professional
Belgium (Flanders)	Professional	Professional	Professional	Academic	Academic	Academic	Professional
Canada	Professional	Academic	Both	Academic	Academic	Academic	Academic
Chile	Academic	Academic	Academic	Academic	Both	Academic	Both
Colombia	Academic	Academic	Academic	Academic	Academic	Academic	Academic
Denmark	Professional	Professional	Professional	Academic	Both	Academic	Academic
Estonia	Unspecified	Unspecified	Unspecified	Unspecified	Unspecified	Unspecified	Unspecified
Finland	Unspecified	Unspecified	Unspecified	Unspecified	Unspecified	Unspecified	Unspecified
Germany	Both	Academic	m	Academic	Academic	Academic	Both
Israel	Unspecified	Unspecified	Unspecified	Unspecified	Unspecified	Unspecified	Unspecified
Italy	Unspecified	Unspecified	Unspecified	Unspecified	Unspecified	Unspecified	Unspecified
Japan	Both	Both	Both	Unspecified	m	Unspecified	Both
Korea	Both	Professional	Both	Both	Both	Professional	Both
Latvia	Professional	Professional	Professional	Professional	Professional	Professional	Professional

	Early childhood teacher	Primary school teacher	Nurse	Medical doctor	Engineer	Lawyer	Accountant
Lithuania	Both	Both	Both	Both	Academic	Academic	Professional
Luxembourg	m	Professional	Professional	Both	Both	Academic	Both
Netherlands	n.a.	Professional	Both	Academic	Both	Academic	Academic
New Zealand	Unspecified	Unspecified	Unspecified	Unspecified	Unspecified	Unspecified	Unspecified
Norway	Unspecified	Unspecified	Unspecified	Unspecified	Unspecified	Unspecified	Unspecified
Slovenia	Professional	Professional	Professional	Academic	Both	Academic	Both
Sweden	Unspecified	Unspecified	Unspecified	Unspecified	Unspecified	Unspecified	Unspecified
Switzerland	Academic	Academic	Both	Academic	Both	Academic	Both
Turkey	Professional	Professional	Professional	Professional	Professional	Academic	Academic
United Kingdom (England)	Academic	Academic	Academic	Academic	Both	Both	Both

Note: m. missing, n.a. not applicable
Source: OECD Data collection on professional tertiary education.

www.ingramcontent.com/pod-product-compliance
Lightning Source LLC
Chambersburg PA
CBHW082344220526
45470CB00008B/2637